THE PATTERN OF POLITICS

THE MACMILLAN COMPANY
NEW YORK · BOSTON · CHICAGO
DALLAS · ATLANTA · SAN FRANCISCO

MACMILLAN AND CO., LIMITED
LONDON · BOMBAY · CALCUTTA
MADRAS · MELBOURNE

THE MACMILLAN COMPANY
OF CANADA, LIMITED
TORONTO

The Pattern of Politics

The Folkways of a Democratic People

By J. T. SALTER

ASSOCIATE PROFESSOR OF POLITICAL SCIENCE
UNIVERSITY OF WISCONSIN

NEW YORK

The Macmillan Company · 1940

Copyright, 1940, by
THE MACMILLAN COMPANY.

Set up and printed. Published September 1940.

FIRST PRINTING.

PRINTED IN THE UNITED STATES OF AMERICA
AMERICAN BOOK—STRATFORD PRESS, INC., NEW YORK

FRONTISPIECE

Know Thyself.

*   *   *

"My people are destroyed for lack of knowledge: because thou hast rejected knowledge, I will also reject thee . . ?" —Hosea 4:6.

*   *   *

"Mr. W: Just a moment. Did Codreanu ever attain power?

"Professor Pickup: No, poor chap, on the contrary, he . . .

"Mr. W: If that is the case, let us ignore him, since we are not dealing with poetry but with politics."—*The School for Dictators* by Ignazio Silone, p. 258.

*   *   *

"It is precisely that outcome of intergroup conflicts which the democratic politicians shield us from. If they sometimes lie in the strenuous task, it is regrettable but understandable. If they sometimes truckle, that is despicable but tolerable. If they are sometimes bribed, that is more execrable but still not fatal. The vices of our politicians we must compare not with the virtues of the secluded individual but with the vices of dictators. In this context, almost beautiful things may be said of our politicians—by way of compensation, if not by way of extenuation, of whatever vices attend upon the arduous process of saving us from violence and murder."—*The Promise of American Politics* by T. V. Smith, pp. 248-249.

ACKNOWLEDGEMENTS

My list of acknowledgements is necessarily a big one. For writing about politics is taking life for my subject. I rarely talk about the weather. I forestall that topic by asking my companions' opinions on politics. And my companions—even if companions only for an hour—range from the creative thinkers at the top to the citizens at the bottom who sometimes are too busy to vote. This fluid group of people with whom I discuss politics is as wide as it is deep. There are clergymen and gentle people on the one hand, and at least one Irish politician (now confined within prison walls) on the other. The variety of people with whom I have talked, regardless of the level on which they live, have demonstrated to me how profound the general interest in politics is on all sides today. (A student working on one of my surveys of opinion knocked on a voter's door. The voter listened a moment and then said, "I don't know what you want, but hell, bud, if you want to talk politics, come in!")

I thank each one for his kindness and intelligent interest in talking to me. These discussions invariably had freshness, life, and color, qualities descriptive of politics and politicians, and—unless I have woefully failed—of this book. Even though I do not here attempt to thank individually these most kind and cooperative people outside the university walls, I salute them as a priceless group.

However, my university colleagues are "special," and I

cannot forego expressing my thanks to some of them—to Professors William Ebenstein, Harold Groves, Walter A. Morton, Edwin E. Witte, R. Wallerstein; to Mr. Alfred P. Fernbach and Mr. E. W. Mill; and to one on the fringe of the campus, Rabbi Max Kadushin. I also thank Miss Emily Blenis for her willingness to type and re-type my manuscripts—some seven times. My greatest obligation is to my better half—my wife, Katharine Shepard Hayden. Her wisdom and poetic insights have helped me—sometimes, it is true, only after a verbal battle—on many questions. Talking is a pleasure—and talking to her is the chiefest pleasure I know.

I am grateful to the editors of the Journal of Politics, the American Political Science Review and the National Municipal Review for their generous permission to reprint with modification some of the materials contained in this volume.

INTRODUCTION

This is a book about the very crux of the democratic process. It describes the life force of our politics. If the thing I describe is sound, our democracy cannot fail; and if it is weak, we cannot long survive, even though our administrators, mechanics, machines, and roads are the finest in the world.

This is a book that had to be written, and written in my own way about the things that I think are of first importance. Some people think a different set of matters are of first importance. My wisest cousin wanted me to write about the urgent need for the short ballot in all our governmental divisions. One of my friends suggested that I prepare a tract on the comparative value of different types of road surfacing used in the more than 3000 counties in the United States.

But it is my idea that one might know the number of miles of paved and unpaved roads in the United States, the miles of concrete, macadam, asphalt, gravel roads, rubber, iron or wood block, as well as the number of miles of unimproved roads; and yet, unless he had some specialized position, he might find this knowledge of painfully limited value, to say the least. He might know the constitution of the United States and the forty-eight state constitutions; he might have briefed all the Supreme Court cases (if he were to live long enough); he might know how much lumber, pork, and wheat we produce annually; he might know the tax law for all the taxing agencies, and why some taxes are delinquent and others bear too heavily on real estate; he might know the amount of money spent on education, and the number of children in the sixth grade; or he might even know all the facts in the Encyclopædia Britannica— and yet, with all this in his head, nevertheless he might still be academic in the worst sense of that word so far as his knowledge of our living democracy is concerned.

This book is about the life of a people—their talk, their attitudes, their opinions, their politicians, their leaders, and about themselves—the voters. It does not tell all of that life. There should, for example, be thorough-going chapters on organization, symbols, and money. They will be more adequately presented in a later edition. (The question of money is most difficult. In fact, no one has ever found an adequate answer to the problem of how to finance our political campaigns. It seems that if a political campaign is of interest to all, everyone should participate in paying for it. If it is wrong for a woman to accept a fur coat from a casual acquaintance, it is just as wrong for a party to accept a huge contribution from one or a few of our 130,000,000 people, and permit the others to give nothing.)

The Pattern of Politics is based on the idea that there is a pattern of life—a pattern of life that includes, along with politics, love and religion, the other two things that men think a lot about. If life is likened to a wheel, politics, love, and religion are at the hub. And now, because we have the social service state and because government increasingly reaches out touching our lives, and we are hourly more dependent on it, politics covers more of the hub than ever before. And just as all of the spokes of a wheel start at the hub, so do all of my chapters start with the voter and his politician and return to them. This is why I may repeat the same idea in discussing different aspects of the same subject.

I have written here about certain basic things concerning our politics—things like ethics, talk, "of the people," nationality, religion, and leadership—all of which are parts of political bedrock. This book is, I hope, an expression "of the people." The reader must judge whether my eye has been blurred or my pen has been less than true. It is my aim to make this, *The Pattern of Politics*, serve as a mirror, and my hope is that the subject will do as a lady does when she glances in her mirror before going out. If anything is found amiss, a touch here, or the pat of a curl there, or maybe powder for a nose—and the loveliest woman is even lovelier. And if the voter gets an impression here that will enable him better to see his enormously important task in judging general results and voting for candidates who are for the common good, the future will be secure.

*   *   *

The other day an "Aryan" refugee from Germany put the difference between the totalitarian states and the democracies in these words: "In Germany the assumption is always against you to begin with. You are considered indecent until you are proved decent. In England" (from which he had just come) "you are assumed to be decent until you are proved indecent."

Even at the risk of saying here what everyone knows and what I have written elsewhere, I want to repeat that I am describing life in a free country—a country that has been free since the beginning, since the first settlers arrived at Plymouth Rock. This country and its free institutions are threatened now by a savage force that is destroying life, property, and the rights of man in the nations of Europe. Today Czechoslovakia, Norway, France, and the others have fallen. Our great sister-democracy England— in a fundamental sense the mother of democracy—alone remains. She is fighting for her life. As she is threatened, the United States is threatened; and the more we are threatened, the more I am convinced that our democratic way, notwithstanding its shortcomings, is the best possible way that man has found to guarantee the well-being of a people. It is the only form of government under which the people generally, without respect to race or religion, are free to be decent, are free to be themselves.

Today we are faced with a magnificent and colossal challenge. To survive this crisis and to maintain our integrity we must have courage, moral stability, the capacity to stand on our own feet, the willingness to sacrifice to the bone, and the wisdom to serve the common good of our own free will. And if there still be any who say that one vote is not important, let him remember that a million times zero is still zero, but a million times one is a number of tremendous size.

CONTENTS

THE PATTERN OF POLITICS

CHAPTER I
ETHICS AND THE VOTER

"Public Morality begins at Vinegar Bend."
—The Honorable Pat Harrison

The text above is but one of many that might be used in a discussion of a moral theme that touches the life of man as squarely and as inevitably as the falling rain touches the sea. I begin with the Senator's remark, however, because it is bed-rock, and most of my ideas go back to it. Formerly the great writers in our democracy wrote of human nature and politics; now it is enough just to say "human nature." The two cannot be separated. They are one. The pattern of politics is fashioned out of the attitudes and values of the men and women who vote.

Who are the American voter's heroes? What sort of person is the voter himself and what sort of person does he vote for? What is his code of ethics? What is his attitude toward law? How does he "play the game"? What kind of country does he live in? Are the ethics of university students like other people's? What are the differences between public and private morality? To what and to whom are the American voter and politician loyal?

It is questions of this sort that I shall discuss here. Because of the exigencies of language I shall have to deal occasionally in generalities—to which there will always be exceptions that come to mind. What I am trying to dis-

cover is the norm—the thing that is true for the run of
American voters.

The life of a people cannot be described in a sentence,
but probably something of a people's flavor and direction
can be discovered by looking at its heroes. With us, in this
country, Abraham Lincoln is unrivalled, but there are lesser
heroes too that include George Washington, Thomas Jefferson, Theodore Roosevelt, and Woodrow Wilson. (And
then on a different plane are Jesse James, Will Rogers,
—Lou Gehrig or the current baseball hero, Mickey Mouse,
Charlie McCarthy, and a passing galaxy of movie stars that
add to the gaiety of life for millions.)

The one characteristic that all of these major heroes had
or have in common is the ardor with which they undertook
great enterprises for the people. Our heroes out of the past
were all strenuous Americans. They were either soldiers or
politicians, or both. They were men who did not permit
their respect for law to stay their hand when forthright
action was needed. Abraham Lincoln, our greatest American, had one paramount interest—all else was secondary.
He saved the Union. George Washington led his countrymen in their fight for independence. His problem inevitably was to meet force with force, strategy with superior
strategy. His task at this point was in a region beyond law.
Thomas Jefferson bought Louisiana, but he was doubtful
about the constitutionality of his act. One of his advisers
remarked that the less said about the constitution, the better. Theodore Roosevelt typified the American to an uncommon degree. He said, "Damn the law, I want the canal
built." Woodrow Wilson was a teacher of constitutional
government, but when he was a candidate for governor,
he said, "If you elect me I will be an unconstitutional gov-

ernor." And a more transient hero, a thrice-elected mayor of Chicago, who returned from Europe during prohibition, launched his campaign in our second city with the declaration, "I am wetter than the middle of the Atlantic."

All of these men believed in a liberal interpretation of the constitution. Theodore Roosevelt said that the federal government had the power to do anything that the needs of the people demanded. Always the idea is: This is an emergency. Prompt action is called for. The law does not quite cover this situation, but I cannot permit that fact to prevent me from protecting the people's interest.

The cardinal point in all this is that the American is a pretty big pumpkin. He has colossal faith in himself. *He has a sense of ego,* but *not a sense of state.* Here people and institutions are fluid or mobile—(and in that fluidity lies the hope of democracy). There is an American proverb, "From shirt sleeves to shirt sleeves in three generations." We have no hierarchy of classes, and therefore no hierarchy of values. Politics is the much-heralded domain of equal opportunity, the Horatio Alger story come to life. Any candidate is worth any office he can get. The fact that institutions are not congealed means two things: (1) There are ideals in our democracy but these ideals are in a state of flux—ideals like liberty, tolerance, rights of labor that have not yet in many cases been embodied in fixed institutions. Hence we have what may appear to be a disrespect for law, disrespect for institutions. (2) These ideals are embodied in men—in heroes. This habit of looking to individuals instead of institutions leads to this difficulty—that the admired individual (who may not happen to be a hero at all) may become more important than the law.

Nearly everything here emphasizes the element of the

particular. A problem arises: it is up to the individual. There is no pattern, no set rule as there is in England and in much of the old world. In England one hears that a thing is done or it isn't done. One never or rarely hears this in the United States. Edward VIII did something that isn't done. Kings of England do not marry commoners who have been divorced. There is no law against it. It just isn't done. There is no opportunity to decide this as a particular case. It must be decided by precedents and the pattern that exists. Individual actions in England are part of something bigger than any individual—something that has been stabilized and fixed into a pattern. It is quite easy to see why the Englishman's attitude toward law is different from the American's. The weight of his history, the nature of his social arrangements, and the moral climate make it different. One consequence of this pattern is that in England the rulers are usually taken from those of birth and wealth; but in the United States anyone can be a candidate. In England it is traditional for the great families to serve the state. (The fact that it is a great family is one reason why it serves the state.) The Pitts, the Cecils, the Chamberlains, and the Churchills come to mind.

In the United States the situation is different. Here if one family serves the state for twenty years you are apt to hear a voter say: "We need a change. He has been feeding at the public trough for twenty years." Here it is a matter of getting more votes than the next fellow. And getting these votes is a particular, an individual problem—a matter that depends, most of all, on a flair for getting votes. It may not depend at all on birth unless that birth is very low. The first line in Jim Farley's autobiography reads, "Perhaps half the youngsters of America had a childhood similar to my own." In the preface of Busbey's *Uncle Joe Cannon,* that great Speaker of the House says, "I am one of the great army of mediocrity which constitutes the majority. . . . All my experiences have been as an average man."

Nor need the candidate's success in politics depend on wealth, character, or educational training. It is a problem, pure, but not simple—one involving chiefly one's native wits and ability to get on with people. It is an art comparable to the art of wooing a lady. The American politician like the American voter is the apotheosis of the particular. And because there is this emphasis on the particular—the individual—there is more color and dramatic incident in politics here than in England. For here an issue cannot be resolved within the framework of a pattern or prearranged code. Each issue takes on its own color. It bears the imprint of an individual, not an institution. The direct primary intensifies this emphasis on the individual and on color. This may account for the presence of a preponderant number of individuals with bright markings in our legislatures and other public offices. For if getting elected means getting the most votes, and if you must get a person's attention in order to get his vote, great emphasis will inevitably be placed on getting attention, and on attention-getting devices, ranging all the way from the Hill-Billy band of O'Daniels in Texas and the candidate for sheriff in Kansas who paraded the streets with two full-sized bloodhounds and said that he was prepared to sniff out crime, to the candidate for Congress in Wisconsin who campaigned with a cow and promised the voters a barbecue. (He later gave them a barbecue, but it was provided by a steer. The election-winning heifer was turned out to pasture.) The Big Bill Thompson campaigns in Chicago employed cowboys and cowgirls, torch singers and hula dancers, donkeys and horses ridden by stooges with appropriate placards, and two live rats in a cage placed on the stage of the Cort Theatre where Big Bill talked to the people in downtown Chicago. In the 1940 spring campaign William F. (Sir Launcelot) Gailing put on a full suit of armor, climbed atop a First Ward rubbish box in the heart of the Loop and said, "My life was threatened when I announced I was going to run for committeeman of this ward." He got attention. A candidate (unsuccessful) in Wisconsin stood on a high porch above the crowd and drove ten-penny nails in a plank for all to see, saying he was building his platform. A successful candidate for city council in Tulsa, Oklahoma, addressed a meeting of several hundred Negroes by walking to the platform, rolling a pair of dice on a desk in full view of all, and saying, as the ivory cubes left his hand, "Here is the only thing I want to tell you folks." Finally, there is the candidate in the East who spoke to the voters by writing his message from an aeroplane on the ceiling of the sky.

Because the American thinks of himself as a particular case, not confined within any system of rules, there is a tendency here toward anarchy, a tendency toward lawbreaking. Anyone who has laughed at Charlie Chaplin and W. C. Fields at the movies probably has something of this tendency in him. In many of his films Charlie Chaplin (the hero) is fighting the police. However, it invariably happens that he is fighting for some value above the one that the police are trying to protect. In these contests the American audience is with Chaplin or Fields in their antics—against the police. The typical American attitude in this connection was expressed at a meeting of a group of business men who were talking about sending money to Finland. One asked, "Is it constitutional?" Another quickly replied, "What difference does that make? We want to help those Finns."

* * *

In this country, sovereignty resides in the people. The state is a servant—a means to an end. That end is the citizen. The supreme law of the land is the constitution; and this constitution throws up a bulwark around a domain wherein the lone individual American is free from all government and law. The American is especially interested in this bill of rights that guarantees him freedom of speech, freedom of press and assembly, and freedom of religion. The fundamental law can be changed with great difficulty. It has been formally amended only twenty-one times in our entire history under the constitution, although our Supreme Court has, in a characteristically American way, amended it countless times. However, when the constitution no longer meets the needs of a controlling number of people, it is either (1) changed, cf. the 18th Amendment, or (2) ignored, cf. the 15th Amendment.

When the American breaks a law (and many laws are broken and certain laws are broken many times) he is usually bent on getting *more* freedom. The American basically resents being interfered with, even though our legislatures are endlessly enacting laws. (Man has long been interested in gambling, prostitution, and liquor, and some governments do not prohibit these activities. The American governments sometimes do, and so whether or not their laws will be obeyed will depend on the background and taste of a controlling number of people in a given community.)

And that is why each community is a law unto itself. The wants of the people in a given area determine, within broad limits, the laws that are obeyed (and enforced too). However, an American would not permit law-breaking that would take away the writ of habeas corpus, or deprive him of his personal freedom. As I have said, law-breaking that is habitual here, and even accepted in some quarters, is most likely to be of the sort that gives the individual more freedom, not less. No man can read the future, but a concentration camp is as foreign to our thinking and our history as would be the proposal to deny the ballot to Protestants.

Our citizens can and do stand as individuals. We have less need for outer props than do the great majority of people elsewhere. We can act singly, individually, and alone. We do not need a class, or a convention, or a bund, or a black shirt to support us. We know that one black shirt or a million of them is still a black shirt. The brain is somewhere else. We are interested in having and using our own brains, in asking our own questions, in making our own decisions. Again I say that here the lone individual is important. He does not surrender his sovereignty lightly. The American may lose his vote through a false promise or a misleading smile. But with the exception of the colored people in the South, and certain submerged groups who are unfamiliar with democratic processes, he has rarely lost it through violence. In other words, here as elsewhere, before you can have a voter, you must first have a man, and when you have a man in this country, you have an individual and a free vote.

The average American really believes that "honesty is the best policy." That is an American proverb that, so far as I know, does not exist in any other language. It is the American idea that it is smart to be honest. And this is the reason why he is mainly honest; it is not because he has a sense of sin. His chief thought, though, is to get on, and if he can once get on, he is confident that the rest will be added to him. He believes in fair play, but he is enthusiastic about success. He plays the game hard, and he wants to win. He passively respects the good, but he positively loves the colorful personalities even though their goodness may be suspect.

The American is not obsequious. He lacks a sense of reverence. Foreigners are amazed when they first come to this country and hear the lowly Nobody discuss his President or lesser public personalities. To hear some citizen or the *Chicago Tribune* talk about Franklin Roosevelt one might think that the man who carried forty-six states in the 1936 election is now wanted by the police. Then the foreign observer will learn that one of the rights of the American is to tell anyone in public life to go to hell if he wants to— (not to his face, but in conversation about him, or in the newspaper). There is a lot of this hate in America, but it tends to be evanescent. Blowing off verbally seems to ease it.

Sometimes the American thinks of himself as omnipotent. Whether he be a mere policeman at $4.00 a day, or an alderman, or governor, he may think of a government as his tiny domain or as his personal property to do with as he thinks best. Hitler and the dictators abroad, of course, have carried this idea to an extreme that is foreign to our experience here, and although the two views differ only in degree, yet to compare them is like comparing an Old Town Canoe with the Deutschland. Some years ago when Fred Zimmerman was governor of Wisconsin, he campaigned in New York City. He was with some friends in a Ford, and they pulled into a one-way street and stopped. Along came a big Irish policeman. He said: "There's no parking on this street after seven o'clock." One of Mr. Zimmerman's friends got out of the car and said: "But, officer, when you got the Governor of the State of Wisconsin in the car, can't you forget the parking ordinance?" The great Irishman's attitude changed in a flash. He smiled and said, "And sure, all the courtesies of the State of New York are extended to the Governor of Wisconsin, and the automobile stays right here." The Irishman was just a policeman, and yet he extended all the courtesies of the State of New York to Mr. Zimmerman. And, incidentally, these courtesies were just as real as though a constitutional convention or a state legislature had acted on the question as to whether the Governor of Wisconsin's automobile could park in a one-way street.

Another illustration of a public official looking upon the state as his private preserve occurred in March 1939 when Governor Moore of New Jersey appointed Frank Joseph Hague, Jr., an allegedly incompetent person with a magic name, to the state's highest bench at a salary of $9,000 a year. The Governor said: "*I know this appointment will make his dad happy.*" Here is the attitude in a nutshell. The boss makes a man governor, the governor appoints the boss's son, or anyone else that the boss designates, to a most important place, and then he says, "This will make his dad happy." He doesn't say, "He will be a great judge," or that "this will make the state of New Jersey happy," for he sees the whole thing in terms of a single individual, often when the single individual unfortunately has no real or theoretical claim whatever to special consideration.

Here is a police chief who disregards the court's interpretation of the law and substitutes his own. The supreme
court in Everystate declared Bingo games to be gambling
and to be contrary to the law of the state. The chief of police in the capital city immediately thereafter said that he
would not enforce the law against gambling when churches
or fraternal organizations carried on Bingo games, but he
would enforce it in case some purely commercial organization undertook to operate Bingo games. Again you have
the individual who sees the situation, not according to a
pattern or set of rules, even though the rules were announced by the supreme court in this case, but as he, a reasonable man, would see it. It obviously points to a lack of
respect for law. These illustrations stand for millions of
comparable ones, in which the individual is the thing, not
the law.

* * *

America is a land of paradoxes. For one thing our annual
crime bill has been variously computed from six or eight
to fifteen billions each year. Probably more murders, rapes,
and robberies are committed in one of our large cities in a
year than are committed in all of England. When Al
Capone was arrested, he owned one state senator and how
many other public officials I do not know. And yet, in
spite of our kidnappers and our other criminal population,
in spite of our insane in institutions, and those on the luna-
tic fringe, nevertheless we have, I believe, more people
using freedom in a humane, constructive, and creative way
here than has any nation on earth.

I am not unmindful of the strong claim that Switzerland
and the pre-Hitler Scandinavian countries can put forth to

this distinction. However, to consider one main aspect, in most of the old countries there was, comparatively speaking, no adventure ahead, no great freedom to chart a new course of the kind there is in the United States. One knows what his profession or occupation is; and he knows the people that are above him as well as those who are lower down; and it probably was the same with his father and his father's father. And if it were not for the uncertainty caused by war and the possibility of revolution, he would be secure in his unchanging status for the whole span of his life.

But here the future is illimitable. The position a person holds today does not necessarily throw any light on the place, education, or wealth held by his father, or other ancestors, or any light on the future either. It always has been an individual proposition here. At the moment, of course, the future looks dark to many. There is great uncertainty; and a man may well be restless. But he is not going to starve. The government provides him with food if he cannot get it himself. He is free to talk and vote and travel as he will. He belongs to himself. And what he will do for that self is his problem. He might know that the economic aspect of this problem is an object of greatest concern to the most brilliant minds in government and the world of research. The answer has not yet been found. The American has not gone this way before, but he has a strong hunch that he will not fail. He may be down, but he isn't out. Nowhere does Hope burn so brightly in the human breast as in America.

Our freedom here is social as well as political and economic. One indication of it comes up by contrast when a question such as this is asked: Who hunts in England? The landed gentry—the people of wealth. Who hunts in the United States? Anyone strong enough to draw a bead and pull a trigger. I know a farm boy who has just gone to Alaska looking for work. He does not have an extra dime. Yet he killed two polar bears his first three months there. Men on WPA or boys in CCC camps hunt deer in Wisconsin. Actually anyone can hunt. Stories have been written about the Negro and his traditional coon hound. In America wild game is wild and free like the stars. It belongs to no man. Poaching is not in our lexicon.

*   *   *

The United States is more than forty-eight states, 3,065 counties, and some 130,000,000 people; it is this, but it is more than this. It has twelve major sections, and some of these sections are outwardly as different one from another as Africa is different from Switzerland. Moreover, these sections, in addition to having their own distinguishing color, occupations, and culture, are further subdivided into an untold number of natural communities and neighborhoods. For example, according to the 1930 federal census, there are five cities each containing more than 1,000,000 inhabitants, and at the other extreme are 13,443 towns or rural areas of less than 2,500 and accounting for 53,820,223 people, or 43.8 per cent of our population. I will not discuss the recognized differences in the mores and habits of urban and rural dwellers, but I will say that the city person must be more alert than his brother in the country, or he will get run over. Now in addition to this great division between the rural and the urban are other differences, of an even more telling nature, in the composition of our population. There are Negroes here, and in some states a majority of the population is colored, and they may be either discouraged or prevented from voting. According to the 1930 census there are 14,204,149 foreign born Americans among us, and 32.3 per cent of our people are foreign born or the children of foreign born, including those of mixed parentage. Furthermore, there are 49 Americans whose income in 1937 was above $1,000,000 and 12,318 persons with incomes from $50,000 to $100,000, and on the other side the lowest third of the population have incomes of not more than $750 a year. This is a hint of the differences that exist in our population of more than 130,-000,000. Not only do the people, and in some cases their language, idiom, and accent, in one major section, differ from those in another, but in a city so small as 100,000 there are a number of communities, and an even greater number of neighborhoods, and the values and ideals and habitual practices in one may be as different from those in another (even though both neighborhoods may be in the same city) as an illiterate miner may be different in his tastes and code of values from a rector of the Episcopal Church. Each neighborhood, in many intimate and profound ways, may be a world of its own. And if great differences exist here, how much greater are the differences likely to be when different communities in the same state, or in different states or sections, are compared.

Just one indication of the differences in problems and in attitudes in the various states is reflected in the statistics on lynching. From 1882 to 1938 one person was lynched in Delaware and one in New Jersey; but during this same period 568 individuals were lynched in Mississippi and 517 in Georgia. The other states range somewhere in between. For example, New York State had two lynchings in this period and Texas 486. The total number in all of the states is 4,687, of which 1,289 were white and 3,398 were black.

Divorce and its status is another point in question. It is a basic institution that is not recognized by any law in South Carolina, but in Idaho or Nevada a person may obtain a divorce after a residence of six weeks. In Massachusetts the residence for divorce is three years, while in the majority of states the residence period is one or two years. There are other basic differences in the laws of the various states concerning marriage and divorce.

The point of all these statistics is merely to emphasize the fact that it is impossible, save with very broad strokes, to describe the American voter. However, he must be described if one speaks seriously of the American politician. For the two together go to make up this great subject, politics. Therefore, while I am describing the voter, I am also aware that there are endless exceptions to my statements. But the reader will, I hope, get a clearer picture of himself and of other voters by noting the pattern which I have sketched of our people—and which determines the quality and bent of our politics.

*   *   *

Political mores, like divorce, are indicative of the tone and quality of a community. The laws on various subjects vary more than do the customs of the people, but customs and attitudes vary too. Kentucky, for example, I think, is unusual for its violence at election time. I do not know how many men have been killed there during campaigns and balloting since the turn of the century, but I imagine that the number is greater than in any adjacent state, possibly than in any other state. I know that they only recently repealed a law requiring the ballots to be kept in cold storage for twenty-four hours after election day before they could be counted. This presumably was to give the angry passions of the candidates a chance to cool. I also know that in certain parts of the land of Hatfield and McCoy, school teachers (of either sex) are asked to stay indoors on some election days lest they be shot. Everystate, in contrast to such states as Kentucky, has enjoyed, until very recently, the reputation for having singularly good government. It has been outstanding in its awareness of the people's needs. Its biggest city is so well managed that it is sometimes spoken of as the best governed big city in America. Yet in Everystate there are many communities: some are more interested in law observance than others. A rather typical community has been described by a prominent newspaper as "spineless and gutless" because it permits slot machines and other gambling devices to operate contrary to law. A public official there privately explained his community's attitude toward law by saying, "It is a lake resort city. The resort people believe in wine, women, and song. . . . Because of the added trade these people bring, laws cannot be enforced too much in minor details or this trade will be driven away."

This comment is characteristic. It reminds one of Ibsen's play, *An Enemy of the People*. When a community must choose between its financial profits that it can see and feel here and now, and a true respect for law whose real implications may not be visible at the time, the choice is particularly difficult. If the side of the law is not effectively and dramatically presented by a moral leadership worthy of its name, the law will fail in this clash of interests—the financial versus the intangible idea of law.

The people will ultimately call the turn, of course. The decision is written in their recurring wants and their sense of values. In one corner of Everystate, for example, is a small city—Bowley—of about 3,000 people, mainly miners. This community has eighty-one saloons or taverns, thirty or more sporting houses, and three churches. The largest is Roman Catholic; the others are German Lutheran and Presbyterian. (I should add that gambling is naturally permitted in a community that does not deny houses of prostitution.)

A few weeks ago, as I have said, the Everystate supreme court declared Bingo a gambling game and therefore illegal. In Bowley there was one Bingo game at the time of the decision, but shortly thereafter another game was started, and now there are two. Although the people operating the Bingo games were not bothered by the pronouncement of the high court, they were disturbed by a problem of another sort. In the past they had given groceries as prizes, but the merchants so vigorously protested against this unfair competition that this practice was abandoned. Now the winners in Bingo games get cash instead. It is as simple as that. When someone with a stake in law enforcement gets excited, something is done. As T. V. Smith wisely remarked, the good is near the "goods."

At this point I shall not attempt to describe the people of Bowley (sometimes called the red-light district for a region) in detail; however, I cannot forego describing one experience that may give the reader an insight into the tone of the place.

At a recent mayoralty election, the mayor, who was a candidate for re-election, walked into a tavern where about fifteen men were loafing around. Personal feeling runs high around election time, and seven of these men were bitterly opposed to the mayor. However, His Honor smiled at the group as he walked to the bar, and said, "Come and have a drink." The leader of the "antis" stepped near the mayor and asked, "Who's buying?" The mayor said, "I am." Pfut! went the other fellow. He spat squarely on the mayor's shoes, and just stood and glowered at him. An expression of anger touched the mayor's face for only an instant. He turned to the other men and said, "What will you have?" The opposition group walked into the street without a word. The others drank with the mayor.

I recently talked to a man who had been governor of Everystate. During his election campaign he told the newspaper man, in answer to a query about Bowley, "We are going to annex Bowley to Everystate. We are going to bring it back into the state." And now years later he tells me, "Shucks, we didn't do it. Those people up there, you can't do anything with them. They want that sort of thing. Liquor, women, gambling!"

*   *   *

Not long ago I was deer hunting in the far north. My two most interesting companions were a municipal judge and a postmaster. The first night in camp I asked the judge what the people in Red Lick thought of him. He quickly answered, "They think I am the best natured son-of-a-bitch in town." I then asked if there were not complaints about the gambling in the town and county. He assured me that there were none. The gambling was illegal, but there were tourists in the summer and the people accepted it without question. Several hours later, when I was only on the fringe of the discussion, and the judge and the postmaster were continuing the talk about vice and gambling in their community, the judge said, "You know Father McR—— [a Roman Catholic priest] told me that he could not do anything for the young people so long as Red Lick has these gambling joints."

Here unwittingly the judge had given the answer that I had looked for before. A priest had spoken out, not vigorously, but to the judge. In another community the spokesman may be a newspaper instead of a priest. If it is a newspaper, its power is greater than an individual's is apt to be because it reiterates and dramatizes the lowly or the big lie or steal or bribe. It is so important in arousing and guiding sentiment and opinion that one can gauge a community's attitude toward law and public morality merely by reading its newspapers.

The people of Vinegar Bend, or the people anywhere, are, as I have said, the measure of public morality, but they must have some leadership. People as a whole are variable; they swing all the way from lethargy to violent action. They are capable of being led to great heights and able to put forth sustained action for a common goal; but the mutuality of the goal must be made plain—as a great imaginative novelist makes an idea plain or transparently clear. The truth is not enough, but the truth touched with fire might be—the fire, or magic, or dramatic ability of a leader. "The people," yes—but the people plus their leaders. The actual key to the community may be found in the public figures whom it supports. What actually happens in life is not enough; what is said (or left unsaid) about these happenings may be more important. This is why books like UNCLE TOM'S CABIN may move tens of thousands to act; but Uncle Tom himself may shuffle by unnoticed, until a Harriet Beecher Stowe comes along to "spot-light" him. The secret, I believe, of Mayor La Guardia's strength is a remarkable flair for presenting politics as theater, for acting, dramatizing, making vital a way of life that the people want; but they may not know that they want it until someone makes it seem real and possible to them. Dan Hoan in Milwaukee is another example of this sort of thing, and was for about twenty-four years. He used the Socialist party and its organization to carry his ideas and facts to the people. Not all the people always, for in some campaigns he told the party workers who distributed the Socialist literature, "to skip the boulevards." Cincinnati has achieved good government through a charter committee and through the committeemen's energy and intelligence in organizing the people interested in law and efficient government, just as the boys of Boss Cox and Rud Hynicka were organized for Boss Cox and Rud Hynicka. Mayor Seasongood said that things cannot get any better until they first become very bad. In 1925, when the Charter group took over, conditions were that bad. Now, after a period of excellent government, in 1940 the charter group is less secure; some of the moving spirits in the committee, and the lesser lights too, are tired; but they know what good government costs, and they have not lost it yet; if they do lose it, they know what must be done to get it back.

The problem of achieving good government through good leadership is simpler in a stable community than in one in which great numbers of people come and go. It is simpler too in an area where there is no submerged group, whether it is submerged because of poverty or race. But everywhere the people need not only leaders but infinite persistence and patience to give cohesion to their better impulses. In a very real sense, the problem—and it is a problem—of keeping a community well governed or clean is not unlike my wife's problem in keeping our son Kit clean. He is a year and a half old. He is washed and re-diapered many times each day. He is wrapped in a dry diaper in the middle of the night too. This process of keeping the baby sweet and clean is as continuous as the passing of time. Every day, every week, every month, and for a while, every year. Communities are like that. Elections are just the beginning of this process of good government—never the end.

II

At the finish of my semester's course on Politics and Citizenship, one of my students, who is the son of a state assemblyman, came to me and said, "Professor Salter, your party course is fine, but there is one thing that I want to tell you. Everyone in politics is crooked and that goes for my old man too!" Now to say that all men are everywhere corrupt is like saying that all of the young women in Kentucky are beautiful—though some are. Yet I have no doubt that this hard-bitten junior has sufficient evidence to convict himself and his honorable sire, and probably many voters in his northern district—and other districts too.

This life that is the matrix of politics and ethical attitudes is everywhere about us. All one needs to do is to read, look, and listen. One afternoon I was in the University bookstore when two young students tried to sell some high school texts. The salesman asked if these books had the principal's stamp in them. The boys picked up the books and went out. In answer to my query I was told that the bookstore had to guard against stolen books. Their safe-guard is the principal's stamp. "Every day or so some mother calls the store and says, 'Watch out for Johnnie's books. They were stolen yesterday.'"

A class of students in a state university is a microcosmic bit of life. The background, values, tendencies in this laboratory represent the great society in miniature. This is especially true so far as moral ideas are concerned. Regrettable as it does seem, a youngster is not likely to acquire a vital interest in ethical questions at the university, even though he lives within its ivied walls for four years. If he hasn't any standards when he comes, he is not apt to have any when he goes. The following incident is in point: The examination papers of two girl students were identical. The professor thought he knew the one who had done the copying. He asked her to confess. Finally, she said she would confess if nothing would be said about her case until after Wednesday. When asked, "Why Wednesday?" she replied: "My father is a banker. He comes up for trial on an embezzling charge on Wednesday."

Some time ago a scandal came out during the campaign for electing a prom king. One of the lesser contenders charged that the leading candidate had offered him the job of program chairman if he would withdraw from the race. The next day I met a group of twenty undergraduates for quiz discussion. More than half of the students were girls, and of that number only one said that she would like a date with the boy who had told. All of the other girls were sure that they wanted nothing from him, but thought the leading candidate very nice, and thought that the unfortunate thing about the proposed deal was that it had been found out. This small group's attitude about a moral question in campus politics helps one understand the crowds at the movies in New York who applauded Jimmie Walker and hissed Samuel Seabury right at the time the latter was charging Mayor Walker with having accepted hundreds of thousands of dollars.

At one University library there was about $5,000 worth of books stolen by the student patrons last year. Who the students are, I do not know, but out of some thousands of students, a number could not resist the temptation of taking a book, now and then, from the open shelf. Long ago when I was an undergraduate at Oberlin College I was more than mildly surprised to learn that more books were stolen from the theological library than from the general college library. It seems that people who will not rob a bank, may steal a book. I do not know why our ethical code at this point should be weak, but for some people it is.

The honor system is used in a Texas high school where one of my friends teaches. She tells me that this system does not work there, for the other students will not report cheating. When she asked why they would not tell on a person who cheats in an examination, the reply was, "We are not tattletales." This attitude, and it is not rare, suggests that the thing that some high school students hate is not cheating, but carrying tales, or telling on a classmate. Paper morality may be different, of course, from the morality that is practiced. However, their elders are not always better. Charles Evans Hughes and Herbert Hoover sat in the same cabinet with Harry Daugherty, Albert Fall, and Denby. They said nothing at a time when the need for a strong clear voice was urgent. The Hon. Calvin Coolidge was not far away. It is true that he did not steal the oil, and it is just as true that he said nothing about those that did. William Allen White tells the story about Coolidge when he was at school. One night someone stole the cook stove. The dean asked Coolidge if he had heard the persons taking the stove. Coolidge answered, "Yes." He was then asked why he had not done something about it. Coolidge replied, "It wasn't my stove." A more recent case conerns a member of the stock exchange who took funds and securities of his customers and used them for speculation—and lost them. His friends and associates knew of this member's illegal use of funds. But none of the great financiers felt it to be their responsibility to notify anyone of his wrong-doing. He, the one who did it, is now in Sing Sing. Other members of the Stock Exchange who kept silent are spotless and free.

Or a more pertinent instance from the world outside revolves around a three-cornered fight for a major public office in this country in the last election. The candidate of a major party was elected. However, before the election a candidate for the Senate charged the successful gubernatorial candidate in question with offering him several thousand dollars to withdraw from the campaign. This charge was front page news. It was never established in court. It was denied. It probably was inconsequential in the campaign. The voter was thinking about the low price of butter fat and he would not be bothered by a rumor.

Once I sat with the discipline committee at a great university. The evidence was all in; the committee was reaching a verdict. One member suggested disciplinary probation for the erring student. There seemed to be general agreement, and then some one said, "They say our committee is too lenient." The chairman looked up, "Who said that?" "Professor Geezer." "Oh, so old Geezer is sounding off!" A pause, and then: "Let's expel this student for one term." It was so agreed. The incident made me think of my talks with a district attorney. He said that he could not possibly enforce all of the laws. "In fact, ninety per cent of the law violations I do not bother with." When I asked which ten per cent he enforced, he said those that a newspaper or some other interest told him to enforce.

A few years ago I learned that graft in China is called "squeeze" and that it is a well-established institution. The public expected not only their civil servants, but their domestic ones, to squeeze. The sin there, I am told, is to be found out, or to take too much graft, or to fail to take care of one's dependent relatives. But a measure of graft is recognized as part of the prerequisite of a position. In fact, to graft or to squeeze is a regular verb conjugated:

I squeeze	We squeeze
You squeeze	You squeeze
He squeezes	They squeeze

But China is different from the United States in this. Here graft is never openly approved of or countenanced. It may be suspected, or it may be vaguely known, and the individual is still unembarrassed; but once it becomes an established fact the prestige of the accused falls mightily. Before an indictment, however, and especially before a conviction, many charges, and even some of a most reprehensible character, may be hurled against a winning candidate—and he may still win. Big Bill Thompson said, "If your opponent calls you a liar, you call him a thief, or if the newspapers attack your moral character, you can charge a kept press. The voter will not know what to believe." A person suspected of public dishonesty may continue to move with comparative freedom within his accustomed groove or circle. Mr. X was connected with the Regulatory Commission for a long time. I was told frequently that he was protecting the private interest involved instead of the public. I mentioned the fact to the attorney general and to three other pertinent officials, and all agreed that he was dishonest but that they lacked the necessary proof to remove him from office, since he was under civil service law protection. During all of this time he prospered and greeted the public with a fine open smile. Then the state government was reorganized, and his office was legislated out from under him. Shortly thereafter, a banking securities house closed its doors, surrendered its charter, and its president and vice president were sentenced to the penitentiary. Mr. X was unfavorably mentioned in connection with these officials, and later he was indicted for his alleged failure to make a correct income tax return. To date, August 1940, he has not been brought to trial. Postponement has followed postponement because of his health. Since he has received this publicity pointing to criminal activities on his part, he has spent and is spending much of his time in a hospital. Reputable physicians now declare that his condition is so grave that it is unlikely that he will ever be able to appear in a court room. (I think that Mr. X is dying of publicity and scare.)

This case with its aftermath is but one of many. If all of the facts were known, how many men could be counted whose health collapsed through grief, or who actually destroyed themselves when their dishonesty was made public. The number is so great that the imminence of jail can be reckoned as one of the major causes of suicide. Any mature reader can think of several instances. I cannot easily forget Kenneth Grober, who was a ward leader and deputy coroner in a great city when I knew him. One day, while discussing his life as ward leader, he told me, "It's no cream puff job, professor." A few months later, when he was a candidate for Congress, the storm broke. His opponent delivered sledge hammer blows at him, charging that Mr. Grober had stolen the estates of a great number of poor people and then buried them in Potter's field. During the campaign, Mr. Grober dismissed the accusations by saying that he was not interested in mud-slinging, and that he would discuss issues. The charges, however, were widely and vigorously circulated over the radio and by the press. The public became interested: the congressman who told, however, was spoken of as a rat by the politicians I knew best. Mr. Grober was arrested and brought before the one lady magistrate in the city. She granted him freedom on bail, and held him for a further hearing. When the time arrived for his appearance, and he did not come, the magistrate's telephone rang just as she was on the point of declaring the bail forfeited. A voice over the wire said, "Mr. Grober has just killed himself." The lady magistrate cried.

S. Davis Wilson, the late mayor of Philadelphia, was recently investigated by a grand jury and charged with taking money from gamblers and others. He died in 1939 before he was prosecuted. Oscar Wilde may have prospered at Reading Gaol in spite of scandal, but the politicians that I know and know of were broken by it, once it became known. There are exceptions, as in the case of the convict who was elected to Congress in Minnesota on the plea, "Other men have gone to the penitentiary *after* they have served in Congress. Help me go to Congress now; I have already served my term in jail"—but usually a prison term ends a political career. The freed convict knows that he will never soar so high again. Magistrate X who was also a ward leader was convicted of accepting bribes, was sentenced, and his friends, or many of them, paid to have Mass said for him while he was away. Yet he was not smiling when he came back. Where other ward leaders in this city talked to me with gusto, he was furtive—not only reluctant to talk, but unwilling to be approached. Though some of his colleagues on the city committee may have thought, when he was taken away in the sheriff's van, "There, but for the Grace of God, go I," yet X was the one that went away and X was (and is) the one who suffered. This magistrate and all other ex-convicts know that they will forever more be vulnerable in any campaign. No political party is ever strong enough to sponsor for any important office candidates who have been convicted of public dishonesty. A candidate may weather horrendous charges, but there is something final about death or conviction. As I have said, the American public, though it will tolerate the suspicion of graft, has repeatedly shown that it is usually unwilling to elect convicted men to office.

*   *   *

In what way does public morality differ from private morality? Or are the two the same? I think that the two are different in actuality and that there are several reasons for this. First, in the matter of public morality, the power of government in a sovereign state is paramount. It is free to act just as it chooses. There is no authority above it to hold it in check. This is why we have the spectacle of international lawlessness or anarchy or war at certain times instead of a normal condition of international peace. I think it was Cavour who said long ago that if he and his colleagues had done for themselves what they had been doing for Italy, they would have been branded as bandits and robbers. If that could be said about Cavour, how truly might it be said about the rulers of any number of states today. It takes no additional evidence to support the idea that at the present time the thing that calls the turn in international affairs over a great part of the world's surface is power. Right and good are, in some instances, not only secondary but non-existent in the calculations of dictators. Power is all that counts.

Then, if we consider democratic politics, we are again confronted with the unique place held by government in the life of a people. Lincoln Steffens tells a remarkably good story here. Once some years ago, he was describing the nature of graft in American public life. He was trying to bring out the idea that society actually "offers a prize for evil doing: money, position, power." He then suggested that we take down the offer of a reward. He said, "Let's abolish—privileges." An Episcopal bishop was dissatisfied with the explanations and wanted Mr. Steffens to go way back to the very beginning. The bishop wanted to know who founded this system of graft.

" 'Oh, I think I see,' I said. 'You want to fix the fault at the very start of things. Maybe we can, Bishop. Most people, you know, say it was Adam. But Adam, you remember, he said that it was Eve, the woman; she did it. And Eve said no, no, it wasn't she; it was the serpent, and that's where you clergy have stuck ever since. You blame the serpent, Satan. Now I come, and I am trying to show you that it was, it is, the apple.' "[1]

This story about the apple is significant today because the apple is a prize that the public had, and many private individuals who possess brains, and money, and power want it. The public's problem is to have the apple used so that it will benefit all or the greatest number, but the inducements that private interests can offer for the privileges, franchises, tariffs, police and taxing power that are represented by the apple are great, and the guardians of the public are continually tempted on the one hand to betray or neglect their trust, and often they are denounced by the people anyway (whether they touch the apple or not), no matter how well or ill they conserve the public goods. Therefore, the problem is apt to be an endless one.

A concrete example will illustrate this matter in a very extreme form. Usually the lines are not so clearly drawn as they were in this instance. In 1901 the Select and Common councils of Philadelphia passed ordinances giving valuable street franchises away to favored corporators of new street railway companies. The franchises conferred the right on the companies to occupy several hundred miles of city streets without any return to Philadelphia. Before Mayor Sam Ashbridge signed the ordinances, he received an offer from John Wanamaker of $2,500,000 for the franchises. Mr. Wanamaker had $250,000 spot cash at the time he made the offer as an indication of the earnestness of his proposal. He said that he was not interested in any city passenger railroad corporation and that he offered the $2,500,000 not because he imagined that sum to be the measure of the value of the franchises granted by these ordinances, "for I believe them to be much more valuable, but merely as an indication to Your Honor in concrete form of the magnitude of the gift conferred upon private citizens without return to the people. It seems to me that to give away such franchises for nothing when others stand ready to pay millions for the same rights is little short of public plunder." [2] I know that public indignation in Philadelphia was so high at the time that many citizens wore buttons on their lapels picturing councilmen being hanged, and that groups of citizens went to the homes of politicians to voice their protest. One stormy night a group of several hundred people went to the home of Boss Jim McNichol and pounded on the door until it was finally opened by a boy. He said his father was not home, and voices in the crowd shouted, "Son, your father is a crook." However, in spite of protests, in spite of Wanamaker's offer, the councils passed and the Mayor signed the franchise ordinances and Philadelphia received not one penny. There are other examples that could be cited where even greater public goods were bestowed upon some favored private individual, but as I have said, here the matter was so clearly stated that obviously those who acted against the public good knew that they were doing it, and the public knew it too.

The Seabury investigations high-lighted many of these valuable privileges of New York and the manner in which they were used to serve private purposes. First there were many cases involving the streets. They are the arteries of the city—the privilege of using them is worth millions of dollars each year. This is true regardless of whether they are used for horse cars, street cars, busses, or taxicabs. The owners of busses and taxicabs contend for them. The material uncovered by the Samuel H. Hofstadter Committee revealed public servants who permitted favored bus companies to operate after their franchises had expired, or who

granted franchises to bus and taxicab companies that were
not financially solvent, and denied franchises to companies
that were, and denied franchises to bus and taxicab companies that promised a larger return to the city, and
granted the said franchises to companies that agreed to
give the city a smaller return. Any citizen is bound to ask
"Why," but there was no answer until Seabury asked this
question.[3]

Another privilege or slice of the apple in any city has to
do with the things or materials a city buys. Even though
the thing purchased is ink, there is an opportunity to cheat
the city by buying from a favored dealer at an unreasonable price. So it is with everything the city purchases.
When it is land, the sums involved are often great. The
City Affairs Committee in New York in 1930 made a study
of the land bought by the city for school sites from 1925
to 1928. The committee estimated that the city was losing
$29,000,000 a year from the condemnation proceedings.
Some of the land was bought at thirteen times its assessed
valuation. On all of the land bought during this period the
city paid 3.2 times the assessed value.[4]

New York City owns a number of piers—piers that are
necessary for steamship lines coming into New York. These
piers are not of equal value—consequently they are much
sought after. In recent years, particularly during the
Walker Administration, the steamship company that got
the privilege of using a particular pier often found it ex-
pedient to engage a particular lawyer, and the thing that
counted was more likely to be the fee of the lawyer than
the payment to the city. These, and innumerable other examples, show that the privilege of the public is the thing
that points to the danger spot. It is the apple.

There is another sort of illustration that is exceedingly important and is present wherever a public body fixes rates for a utility—accepts a valuation for a utility of any sort. One street railway company in Cincinnati had obtained all of the laws it wanted, and yet it continued to be "the first and biggest contributor to the corruption of politics here. Steffens asked the manager of the railroad why this was. The manager replied, 'Did you ever notice what our capitalization is?'

"Steffens said, 'Fifty-five millions.'

" 'Well,' he drawled, 'I think—I'm not sure, but I reckon that I could rebuild and reequip these roads for eight or nine—say eleven millions.' 'Well,' he smiled, 'the difference between eleven millions and fifty-five millions is the measure of our—our vulnerability.' " [5]

Of course, one of the most powerful and valuable of the public's privileges is the law. And although Judge Manton is one of the very few federal judges ever to have been convicted of selling the law, yet state judges are more vulnerable, and magistrates—the courts of first instance—are often the most vulnerable of all. Recent testimony of magistrates with great bank accounts and magistrates who have accepted loans from gangsters, or who have bought their places on the bench in New York, support this idea. My investigation of the magistrates in Philadelphia also supports this conclusion.

The principle in all cases involving the public's apple or privilege versus the private contenders for it is the same. But in the magistrate courts the conditions and forces are so elementary that I will describe them in some detail. The flower is brought to fullest bloom in a big city, and preferably where magistrates are elected by the people. Philadelphia is an excellent example—a city of 2,000,000 people who elect 28 magistrates for six-year terms. The 28 elected are never leaders of the bar, or leaders in the broader civic affairs, but they are leaders in their wards, that is, they are ward leaders or politicians who expect to be ward leaders, and they are individuals who, nineteen times out of twenty, have organized support back of them. Now they do not become ward leaders without doing favors, and they do not get the support of the city organization unless they are good party organization men themselves, that is, men who will do favors. The J. P., or Justice of the Peace, courts usually mean judgment for the plaintiff, but in Philadelphia the J. P. means judgment for the politician.

There is a Mr. Michael McManus, who is not a ward leader and not a magistrate, but is one of the personal embodiments of the power of the party organization and the twenty-eight magistrates (save one—the lady that Pinchot appointed when a sitting magistrate died). He is big and jovial and ever willing to talk to a discerning and appreciative audience. He is provided with a small but comfortably furnished office right at the center of things. He has a desk, three heavily-padded chairs, two telephones, and a box of luxurious cigars. His guests are few and select and the mild Havana cigars are part of his Irish hospitality. My introduction was casually given by one of Senator Vare's close friends. We found on subsequent visits that we were both intensely interested in conversation, and particularly in conversation about politics—the wheels within wheels of politics. And as he was one of the wheels and near enough to some of the others to see them turn around, he had much to say that to me had heretofore been discovered only at random, or was mere surmise or rumor.

He was genuinely pleased with the idea that a professor thought his words important enough to copy into his green notebook. Near the end of my stay he said that he too would some day write a book on Magistrates that would be a book of hate and revenge (he always wanted to be a judge himself), but he smiled so charmingly, and he has served Senator Vare and the party, man and boy, so faithfully, for forty-five years, that I am sure he did not mean it although he thought he did. He is so loyal a trooper and so every inch an order man that he has passed beyond good and evil in any matter where the welfare of the party and the work of the magistrates are concerned. Of course he knows that Magistrate Perri did wrongly in 1928 in being convicted of extortion and bribery in connection with the taking of bail; and that exorbitant fees are improper for simple services; and that there is a ward leader's courtesy that extends to him certain privileges gratis for which outsiders may be charged. His attitude makes one think of Lord Bryce's statement: "As respects the defects of criminal procedure in general, it must be remembered that an evil which has become familiar, ceases to be shocking. The standard custom has set, comes to be accepted; it is only the stranger who is amazed."

I will not call Mr. McManus a fixer—that is an ugly term. He is rather one of the contact men. His job is not in the city charter. He is a sort of liaison officer between the leadership of the party and the magistrates. He is an office boy for the leaders. He once told me that his great problem was to know just how far his arm would reach and never go beyond that. "You have a long, thin arm. You don't reach any farther than that arm will reach. I have a short thick arm. Sometimes I reach beyond it. I may go to the penitentiary but you never will."

In ordinary instances in which a person is arrested for some minor law violation he seeks his division leader and the leader sees a magistrate. If the illegal act is more serious, the division leader may take the case to his ward leader. The ward leader may have other engagements or he may be too busy to handle the matter personally; or he may be *persona non grata* to the magistrate in question, so he will do the simplest thing—call McManus on the telephone, give him the facts and let him handle the matter. The magistrate knows McManus, and he knows who he is—the matter is usually attended to. If not, McManus has three other angles from which to approach the problem: (b) the magistrate's clerk, who has charge of the record; (c) a police captain at the station house that can destroy the record; (d) "a personal friend of mine who attends to these things for me. In only one case in fifty does he fail. He is a ward leader and a councilman. These people are obligated to him. They will do what he tells them. Three times in twenty years this connection has changed, but there is always someone there." One day he made the matter very concrete when he said, "Suppose that you got arrested. Smith [leader of X Ward] would call me on the telephone —'Say, the professor was arrested—being held at Manayunk.' We bring down all the powers to bear. Find that the professor is in an awful jam. But I say that since it is less than murder, let him off. The magistrate will. Smith is a producer. Conditions in his ward are terrific.

"I met Smith in Vare's office. The Senator said that he would make him a ward leader. He asked me to give every assistance. We are all one big family. His success is your success and my success. From about 1923–24 Smith has been either coming into my office or calling me on the telephone. He seems to need someone to lean on. I serve him more than other ward leaders because he is weaker and Vare wants to keep him afloat. I am known in the X ward as their attorney."

Late one evening while I was talking to McManus, he called Magistrate W on the telephone. "John, . . . One of my friends has been arrested for selling numbers in a lottery. He has a good moral reputation. He has never been arrested before. . . . His hearing is before you tomorrow morning. His name is ——. Fine. He is discharged already? Won't need to appear at the hearing? Good, John. And say, try to keep his name off the record. Don't want to hurt his character. Goodbye." He turned to me and smiled —"That's not 100 per cent service—that's 1000 per cent service."

On another day the Democratic county commissioner came into the office with two derelicts. "Hello, Mike," said the commissioner. "Hello, Judge," McManus replied. The commissioner then said that one of these men was held for a hearing at nine o'clock tonight.

McManus asked, "What is the charge?"

"Assault and battery," answered the commissioner. "Man beat up his father."

"Was anyone seriously hurt?"

"No."

"Well," said McManus, "give him your card, Commissioner, and he will be discharged."

"Is that all it takes?" asked the commissioner.

"Why not?" said McManus. "Just let him have your card." (The commissioner reaches in his pocket, takes out a book of cards, detaches one, gives it to the man.) A leader has served a constituent; McManus has served the organization.

Earlier in the week I was present while McManus was talking to an elderly Democratic magistrate. The Democrat had been unable to get a desired recognition from a certain other magistrate. McManus said, "You tell me the next time that you want a favor from X. I know the judge. He will do it for me." The leader of a police ward came in, drew McManus aside, whispered in his ear. McManus shook his head, and the leader went out. "When you play politics, you got to be able to say no and yes. Just had to tell X no. One of his people got into a jam. He wanted me to go the limit; I wouldn't do it. Yesterday XYZ (ward leader) made an unreasonable request about Magistrate J. Had to turn him down." He then opened an envelope that contained a summons and an affidavit from a police station. The person named was to appear before a magistrate for traffic violation. On the upper left-hand margin the secretary to an important politician had written in ink the word "please." McManus commented, "You see, M. is down in North Carolina on his vacation."

One of the strongest leaders in the city came in. McManus asked me if I knew him. I said yes, but that he had not talked to me as much as I should have liked. The leader said, "I told you some things and you have to guess at the rest. I can't tell you everything I do in politics." When we were alone again, McManus reminisced.

"Magistrate Blank is very crude and rough. He won't advance in his education. He uses a vile tongue—but he has a good heart. The rough stuff is all on the outside. He argued a point once that X (another magistrate) would not go along on. Magistrate X was interested in this too. I said that I would help—I felt that I should for X was interested in the same thing from another angle. I did, and he thanked me. However, he wanted another favor ten days later. I said that I couldn't do it. 'There is a rule established and I will live up to it.' He replied, 'I want to talk to you about this tomorrow.' 'Come in,' I said, 'but don't talk to me about this matter.' He came in and talked about the same question. Finally I said, 'If I do this you will not know a thing about it. Never even thank me for it.' After I did this Blank said to me, 'If there is anything at any time within my power, call on me, and I will be your club!' I could do what a magistrate cannot do because I have contacts—different contacts.

"I average about ten favors a day done here for the organization and their friends. No compensation for that—only return for that is the welfare of the party. Yesterday a boy was arrested for assault and battery by auto. His mother called me on the telephone. I called the magistrate by telephone; I told him to discharge the boy and keep it quiet. He is a student of La Salle College. If this arrest were made public, it would hurt his record.

"Yesterday I had twelve summonses handed to me to appear before magistrates. These twelve represent five ward leaders. Wouldn't take one of them if they were not ward leaders. The committeeman must see the magistrate for himself."

He showed a note. It ran:

"Dear Mike—I will appreciate your good kindness in behalf of the attached." The name of a ward leader was signed to it.

"My telephone will ring at home. Someone will ask,

'Who is this?' I will answer, 'Who in hell do you want?'
'O.K.,' he will reply, and then we will talk. A ward leader
shouldn't give his name when he wants me to knock out a
rape or some other serious charge.

"I used to keep a record of the services that I rendered
for the party. Here it is." I examined his diary and noticed
the frequency with which the name of the before-men-
tioned ward leader appointed at Vare's suggestion appeared
—twenty-five times between March 4th and the following
June 3rd. And McManus added, "My book shows just one-
sixteenth of what I have done for Smith. Last Tuesday
night at twelve o'clock he called me on a point of law concerning a matter outside of the county. I would do things
for Smith that I wouldn't do for anyone else. Besides, a
regular ward leader like —— would not need to come to me
so often as Smith does."

Earlier that day McManus had told me of helping a
woman who was the wife of a high official in a large public utility. He got her discharged. His friend wanted to
know the cost. McManus said, "There will be no cost. I
do this because you are a friend of mine." He added, "Five
or six weeks ago her husband got lodged in a cell because
of a bad business deal. I was called at 1 A.M. I finally told
his friend that called to have someone take a copy of the
charge to Magistrate V's office in City Hall. This magistrate signed the copy, and the prisoner was permitted to go
home. In the meantime I told the magistrate to let this matter ride until I had had a chance to see him. Next day he
told the man that the hearing would be postponed for one
week. At the time of the hearing, the magistrate called the
man aside before things began and said, 'You are discharged.' The man said, 'I haven't had my hearing yet.'

The magistrate replied, 'What the hell do you care!' The man asked, 'Am I free of this charge?' The magistrate answered, 'Scot free!' My friend came in afterwards and asked me what he owed me. He said, 'This fellow' (the one I had gotten out) 'has plenty of money—he can pay. If he had had an attorney he would have had to pay a fee.' " McManus said, "Why didn't he get an attorney?" The friend said, "Because an attorney couldn't have served him as well as you have." McManus asked, "How much would he have paid an attorney?" The friend responded, "$1,000 would have been a fair fee." McManus said to his friend, "But I did this for you." But the friend said, "You will get your fee." And he got it.

"But," McManus went on, "I don't take graft. Payment for legal services, yes. Graft, no. Look at that." (I looked at a small bundle done up in tissue paper on his desk. He opened it and showed me a necklace of what might have been silver on which was fastened a beautiful cameo the size of a silver dollar—Woolworth or Bailey, Banks and Biddle—who knows?) "A committeeman asked me to do a favor," McManus said. "I agreed. He left his gift behind as he went out. I did not see it until later. I am keeping it here until he comes back and then I will return it to him. Graft—no; but payment for legal service—yes."

Mr. McManus was ever the gentleman; in an apologetic mood he explained that there were many things that he *could* tell me, but he did not care to divulge them. "All evil can be traced to scandal. That is where it originates. My mother told me to build up a character. You can take away money and return it, but you cannot return a man's character. That is why I never say anything scandalous about anyone."

He doesn't—his kindness of soul is genuine. He appears as innocent as a lamb; in spite of his great size he has a disarming humility. I am sure that he is totally unconscious of the social importance of his work. He believes the Roman Catholic church to be the only organization more wonderful and efficient than the Republican party in Philadelphia. His loyalty is inspiring; his social vision is not. He may be described as a super-division leader. He does for the party what the division leader does for his voter. It is only common sense to keep a McManus as long as magistrates, ward committeemen, and voters remain.

The examples above are taken from the life of a great city merely because the stakes are greater—the apple bigger there. And furthermore, it has been simpler because many of the pertinent facts have been dug out and neatly arranged for all to see by endless probes, investigations, and trials. The names of the investigators, Senator Clarence Lexow, Charles Evans Hughes, the Mazet Committee, Samuel Seabury, Thomas Dewey, are sometimes better known than are the public officials that they examined. The apple is truly bigger but so is the floodlight that shows the significance of the values involved in the contest over the apple.

These contests are endless and ubiquitous in our democracy. When I first taught in Oklahoma, I found that one of my mature students would match each of my Philadelphia stories with an Oklahoma story. I said, "So you have a spoils system here?" The student answered, "Yes, the only difference is that we have less to spoil here than you do in Pennsylvania." The basic fact is that every community or rural area—no matter how sparsely settled or poor—has an apple, only it may look like a crab apple to one who has been contemplating the wealth and privileges of other areas. But where there is life, there is politics, and where there is politics, there is an unending struggle between the common good and a private interest. This is why eternal vigilance is the price—not only of liberty, but of good government.

The most acid criticism of public officials, generally speaking, comes from contractors who deal with them. The testimony of Contractor Nunkel who specializes in road work for rural towns throws light on this problem in the country. In some of the rural townships the chairman of the highway committee often expects Contractor Nunkel to use a team of horses instead of a motor patrol when Nunkel builds roads. This is because the highway commissioner may expect Nunkel to hire his team of horses and his son at $12.00 a day for doing the road work, even though a motor patrol is much better than is a team, for pressing gravel. Now some counties require by law that the road work must be done by motor patrol, and Nunkel is buying a motorized unit. He said that he was sure that it would often be idle, and he would be hiring the highway commissioner's team of horses and his son to drive them.

Nunkel works with another man who has the same number of teams and wagons and who carries the same amount of gravel, in other words Nunkel did the same work for the township that Contractor X did. But Contractor X received $700 more from the township. When Nunkel asked him about this fact, Contractor X said that it had cost him $45.00 for a new suit for one of the commissioners in order to get this extra $700. Nunkel had a special plan for members of the county commission who could not be bribed. He provided them with outings up in the Muskellunge country. He would pay all hotel expenses and would give each of them a

quart of whiskey as a souvenir of the trip. The commissioners had come to expect this courtesy from the contractor
and they remembered him when contracts were awarded.
Nunkel also said that he would sometimes drive up into a
commissioner's farmyard and spread several loads of gravel
in the driveway where gravel was needed. Nunkel would
never mention this to the commissioner, and the commissioner would never mention it to him, although if Nunkel
did not do this, the commissioner might remark, "The road
in our driveway is certainly in bad shape, and a load or two
of gravel would help a lot." The county is interested in
having gravel free from sand, and they hire an inspector to
see that it *is* free from sand. This inspector examines the
gravel in the bin and also on the road, but he works for the
county only part of the time, and the rest of the time he
works for Mr. Nunkel, and he is experienced enough to
test the road when it will show gravel and no sand. Items
of this sort are small, but they are apt to be widespread.
They merely suggest again the endless struggle between
the public and the private interest.

One difference in public and private morality is based,
as I have said, on the fact that the government's power is
paramount, and that this power, or privilege, or the apple
is contended for by private individuals for their own, rather
than society's, use. This is only one side of this fact or condition. The other side revolves around the differences that
exist in the servant and master relationship. In private life
the master is one; in public life the master is myriad—one
thousand masters—one million or fifty million.

The servant can talk directly and sincerely to a single
master, but how different is the predicament of the public
servant whose masters are not only ubiquitous, but con-

flicting in their opinions, knowledge, understanding, and intensity. Some of these masters cannot read, many more can read but won't, or cannot understand what the words are worth. The majority have but an eighth-grade education. Many are so preoccupied with other matters that they do not vote. Still others who do vote expect a bonbon of some sort from their candidate. Others will vote for one of their own nationality and religion regardless of the issue. Again some of the masters insist on a personal call from the candidate, or transportation to the polls, before they will effectively tell what they think about the public's business.

It is obvious that a public servant with the multi-master, that is, voters, who both employ and discharge him, cannot speak with candor on all subjects and at all times; to do so would be equivalent to a repudiation of public life. Doctor John Gaus, one of my colleagues, has happily characterized the situation in these words. He said that a parent must consider what he is going to tell his children and what he will withhold from them—not because he is dishonest, but merely because very young people are not ready to entertain all the ideas and opinions that are discussed by their elders. The same thing is true of a clergyman speaking to his congregation. He will not dwell on the questions that come to him. His purpose probably is to bring people to the faith—not to turn them away.

It is certainly true that one cannot speak the truth as freely when he is associated with someone else as when he speaks merely for himself. Furthermore, he cannot speak the truth on all questions when he talks to two or more as he can speak it when addressing only one. This is as true in business as it is in politics. If Gimbel's or Wanamaker's advertise a remarkable rocking chair at $49.50, a salesman em-

ployed by the firm in so describing the product is not likely
to call the chair ordinary, regardless of his opinion. If this
is true in business where only one subject like a chair may
be the subject of the discourse, how much more true is it
apt to be in political affairs where the subject matter may
be as broad as the universe. The reason that political
speeches, party platforms, or any public utterance not limited to some such question as the date of Thanksgiving can
tell only part of the truth about some questions, and not
even mention others is not hard to find. It applies alike to
public officials of virtue and wisdom and to dishonest ones.
The reason is based on the public official's desire to please
—not his intent to deceive.

Or take the case of a cabinet member. The President
makes a statement about foreign affairs or banking, or agriculture; a cabinet member either keeps silent or speaks in
support of the idea, as Secretary Hull did when questioned
about the European trip of Secretary Welles. There must
be countless examples of this sort. The President has ideas
—ideas that surely some of his cabinet members or other
appointees cannot accept. Yet they must accept them,
or resign. If cabinet officers resigned every time they disagreed with the President, the government would be hope-
lessly unstable, or innocuous. Therefore, we accept our
present plan as the better for society, but it does mark a distinction between private and political morality.

*   *   *

The American's attitude toward foreign relations is one
facet through which we see this tendency of the individual
to live in the moment. The American people today are the
hope (and despair) of the world. If there is a flood in

China, an earthquake in Turkey, or a food shortage in Finland, America sends help. She is the richest, most powerful nation in the world and she is able to give help to those who need it, whether they are in Mississippi or Coteshti. Her people are as rich in energy and initiative and the willingness to do the impossible as they are in material resources. The combination tends to be unbeatable.

But America is a curious mixture. She sympathizes with the Chinese and arms the Japanese. She screams at the Communists, but breaks all previous records of exportation to Russia while Finland is being destroyed. She loves liberty, but helps others sneak contraband to Hitler's Germany. She sometimes shouts for isolation, but is enormously interested in European affairs. She gives up her championship of the freedom of the seas, and thereby gives aggressors a free hand to sink neutral ships wherever they may be. At the same time many of her people indulged in violent censure of England for not fighting for Czechoslovakia, Ethiopia, and other victims of the dictators. This paradoxical situation is the result of our diversity, our freedom, and our greed. Some of it may be traced to foreign agents here. America is the happy hunting ground of spies. Here a person, regardless of his nationality, is innocent until he has been proved guilty; furthermore the Americans have other work to do than spy out possible enemies within. We prefer to give the other person credit for his good intentions.

What are Americans actually loyal to? What are they, these paradoxical people, consistent about? Are they loyal to some principle, intangible ideal, or institution fashioned out of human experience, or is this first allegiance given to an individual?

There is no universal answer to this basic question. I

know some people who prefer the truth to any personal advantage wrongfully achieved. These people love the United States, or Wisconsin, or Madison, more than they love any political party, or President, or lesser politicians; but they are almost as scarce as black-tailed deer in the Badger forests. I think the great majority of Americans give their first loyalty to someone or to something concrete.

For one thing, it is so much simpler this way. Who knows what the truth is—or the U.S.A.? And, besides, if we did know the truth or the State, neither the one nor the other could, in the minds of some people, pay us back. Or they could not pay us back here and now. The reason why, to take an extreme case, an individual will sell his vote for cash on election day is obviously that he can see the cash here and now, but cannot see the more fundamental and infinitely greater value for him and all the people, that he destroys. The same is true for the person who gives his vote away for a smile, or for any reason other than the true one—the good of the State.

America is young. As I have already said, this is a growing, changing country. Life is fluid and therefore institutions, and codes, count for less than they do in certain countries of the old world. Our ideals are embodied in men, not in crystallized traditions. The individual man—the Hero, and sometimes the Crook—may be paramount in the loyalties of great numbers of people. At times, indeed, if a principle can get itself embodied in a hero, that principle may hold our loyalty. Jeffersonian democracy may be spoken of more frequently than the principle for which it stands, but it represents a principle. Jacksonian democracy is another example. Woodrow Wilson and the universality of man is still another. Theodore Roosevelt meant the "Square Deal";

Franklin Roosevelt meant "hopeful America" in 1933; in 1934, "the New Deal"; in 1940 he is still a powerful figure in the panorama of American life, but his position is less easily defined.

In each of the foregoing illustrations the man is merged with the principle. His name is used to identify the principle. In 1934, and particularly in 1936, some hundred thousands or millions of voters who favored Franklin Roosevelt were indifferent or hostile to his New Deal program. The idea of a principle or of a state is not one that we readily grasp. In a thousand little daily choices this discrimination against the abstract, the impersonal, is most evident. Not for all the people, I repeat, but for a controlling number. A city manager and a duck hunter in Norman, Oklahoma, once started driving to a convention in Texas. They traveled in the city manager's automobile. Near the end of the day the city manager stopped for gasoline. The duck hunter started to pay for it, but the manager waved his money aside. The duck hunter insisted, saying that now it was his turn to buy; the manager had bought the first tank. The manager said, "Don't be silly, I am on an expense account. This is on Norman." The argument promptly ended.

Later, however, the duck hunter, who was no ordinary duck hunter, thought of the matter again. He saw that his loyalty to his friend had a very different meaning from his loyalty to his city. He decided that one had substance; the other had none. Children under twelve usually ride on railway trains for one-half fare. Suppose a child is twelve or thirteen but looks younger. Is the parent going to ask for a full-fare ticket when he can buy one for one-half the amount? Or suppose a person is traveling on a day coach excursion ticket—the kind that will not be accepted for buying Pullman space. It is late at night in a far away city. The agent carelessly glances at the ticket and asks the traveler if he would like Pullman space. Of course he would like it for the night if he could get it at regular rates, but will he say, "Take another look at my ticket, I do not believe I am entitled to anything but a day coach"; or will he reply, "You bet"?

Jack Benny's income for 1939 was above $250,000. Yet he tried to smuggle goods past the customs to avoid the tax. I have no exact information about the integrity of Rochester's master, but I would guess that he is not the sort of person who would try to cheat a friend in some personal transaction involving money. But to cheat the government—that is different. It's a lark—unless you are caught—and then you look a bit cheap. Only a bit, however, because your public may feel as you do. And Mr. Benny is as funny Sunday evening as though he had treated the government honestly.

The efforts made by many people, and some of the wealthiest, to avoid paying taxes illustrate the matter again. People who would not cheat at cards, or "do in" a friend in a financial transaction may spend anxious hours and thousands of dollars trying to construct a plan to avoid the payment of an income, inheritance, or any other kind of tax. What is more significant, a man who gets around his rightful tax obligation may boast about it. There is no tradition or code to hold the Mitchells in line. In certain relationships and with many people one can beat the government and count it good cricket.

The independence of the voter can lead to slackness in morality. His paramount interest is himself and not the state, or the idea of the state. If this is true of the individual, it is likewise descriptive of the voting legislator—the voter's alter ego. Usually, and most especially in times of peace and prosperity, the voter's problem, and his politician's, in seeing the idea of the state instead of some special concrete benefit to himself, is the same. It is not unlike the problem of the man who closes one eye, holds a silver dollar in front of the other and blots out the sun. The silver dollar is infinitesimally small as compared with the sun, yet it is also infinitely nearer than the sun. A smile or a personal acquaintance is a trivial thing when the good of the state is in the balance. Yet it is so easy to see the smile—it is so near and so warm that one may react to it on the spot. The idea of the state is something far away, unclear, and perhaps uninteresting. Although it is of paramount importance it may not be a controlling factor in the political contest.

As for the actual politicians—those people who have been elected once or twice or more, and count on being elected again—the politicians' first loyalty is invariably to the person or group who they think will have most to do with the next election, and maybe the long future beyond. The politicians usually say that they are loyal to the party, but if they are part of a strong organization, you will find that that is what they are loyal to. If there is a strong leader or boss, the politician's first loyalty goes to him. But if the leader has a stroke of paralysis, or is seriously weakened from any cause, these loyalties are impaired. The cry will be "the leader is dead, long live the leader." And the majority of men will attach themselves to the new boss. In most cases the loyalty of politicians is a loyalty to winners.

A great Speaker of the House once said that in politics

virtue is of less importance than a reliable majority. I do not think that there is necessarily anything incompatible between the two, but one can go to Congress on a majority alone. Uncle Joe Cannon, another great Speaker who had been elected to twenty-three Congresses, was always irritated by reformers who were unwilling or unable to work with other people, and contented themselves with saying, "God and one are a majority." "I always feel like saying, 'My poor simple friend, did you ever stop to think that God is a majority without one?' " Of course, right is right and 10,000 majorities will not stop it from being right, but this does not necessarily have anything to do with the ballots in the ballot box.

The interesting question then is: Just how does a candidate actually get votes for himself into the ballot box? There are two main ways and infinite variations and combinations of these two. John O'Connor, the former Congressman from New York, said that one day Murphy, the boss of Tammany Hall, asked him if he wanted to go to Congress. "I said 'Yes,' and he said I could go. I went." The other main approach is illustrated by the life of the late Senator La Follette. He said that if he could talk to enough people he could win. In his *Autobiography* he said:

"The task of building up and maintaining an intelligent interest in public affairs in my district and afterwards in the state, was no easy one. But it was the only way for me, and I am still convinced that it is the best way." [6]

Now in all cases like O'Connor's (and he is the garden variety of American politician) wouldn't it be odd if his first loyalty were not to Murphy and Tammany? If they could send him, they could certainly retire him. In the case of La Follette, who was rare but not unique in our politics, his support came from the people, and he represented them in Congress.

There is one basic difference between these two types of support. The Murphys, the Rorabacks, and the Crumps, and any other boss or organized group or interest, can easily keep their eye on their own, wherever he may be—and he knows it. It is simpler for one experienced person to follow congressional procedures when he is paid to, than it is for 100,000 amateurs to do so—people who have work of their own to do, shows to see, and countless other engagements to attend to, and only a spasmodic interest in Congress anyway. Besides, the people are away from the scene of action—the implication of the issues confronting their representative on this scene may be outside the ken of many. This basic fact increases the attention that a man in public office will give to any organized part of the citizenry as contrasted with the unorganized or loose or free individuals who speak—if they do speak—for no one but themselves.

Here is the idea in a nutshell. Twenty years ago when Ed Vare was boss in Philadelphia two senators were talking at the state capitol. The Senator from Reading said that he had to get back to the people awhile to see what his constituents wanted. Senator Stanbury of Philadelphia remarked, "I can see my constituents easily. I have only one—Ed Vare."

The action of Governor Moore (cited above) in appointing the boss's son is an example of loyalty. Then there is the cause of Magistrate Stubbs who decided two cases contrary to the merits of each case. A politician lawyer, a friend of the magistrate too, was interested in these two cases. After the hearings, the attorney told the judge that he had decided against him in the case he should have won, and then in the second case, "When the evidence was against me, you decided in my favor." The judge said, "Hell, Councillor, don't you know who was behind that first case? The Senator!" The Senator was the man who had made Stubbs a magistrate, therefore he came first, but no one that mattered was concerned with the second case, except the attorney I am quoting. Therefore he got the decision as a favor. One time a precinct leader told a magistrate how he was to decide a case. The judge was offended at the manner in which the request was made. He angrily shouted, "Who's running this court, you or me?" The ward politician calmly replied, "You are because of the five hundred majority I gave you."

What the judge decided isn't important. The significant thing is the idea that magistrates are elected in Philadelphia, and only those individuals with organized support can normally be elected. Elections of this sort, where the electorate is large and the office small, are apt to mean irresponsible appointments. Therefore, magistrates are likely to look with particular deference to the wishes of the organization, for the organization gave them their jobs. If the candidate had effectively discussed the issues with the people generally, then the magistrate would most probably be concerned with representing some public good; he would be free to decide the question according to the law and evidence. This cannot easily be done if tenure depends on the favor of a private group. The public must assume its own responsibility and, if it is not prepared to do that in the case of elected magistrates, it should arrange for their official appointment.

If instead of the party organization or some other compact and powerful interest, we substitute the words *Gallup*

Poll or the idea of Father Coughlin telling his radio listeners to wire their congressman to vote against the repeal of the embargo, we realize again that the loyalty of a representative may waver. Burke once told his constituents that he would represent their interests against their opinions. He also said that he would represent their opinions, but the opinions they would have five years from today. He refused to be a weather cock. These ideas were eloquently given, but they did not please the voters of Bristol, and they would probably be untenable to the electors in any American district unless the speaker were of unusual stature, like Carter Glass of Virginia or George Norris of Nebraska. But the run of the mine representatives are likely to listen to the voice of their master, and when that voice is clear, action is direct. When there is no voice or when there is a babel of voices, the representative must exercise independent judgment. The foregoing is true because, by the very nature of tenure, the man in public office is bound to love a majority.

A few years ago a happy combination of circumstances enabled a popular and crafty judge to get elected by more than 500,000 majority. An early case in the new term was dealt with by him with such severity that the newspapers vigorously commented on the sentence. The judge promptly answered his critics by saying, "500,000 voters have said that I am right." Actually the five hundred thousand or five million voters had nothing to do with the case. It was a question of law and justice, but one could not discover that by the legal decision or the judicial comment.

Because of the political necessity that makes elected judges dependent on votes for office there is a pliability in some of them—a willingness to sway with pressure. Many of them could say with Shakespeare's Lord Say: "Prayers and tears have moved me, gifts could never." This sentiment may have been expressed by a hundred thousand politicians who will stand for re-election in November 1940, because it is so descriptive of our politician and our people. Although logic has little to do with it, it is obvious that if it is wrong for a judge or any public official to change his decision because of a cash bribe or any other present, it is equally wrong to swerve from the true course of duty because of a prayer or tear. The state cannot cry; the public cannot let fall a tear. Yet they are important parties in any public proceedings even though the common good is invariably sacrificed when tears sway the judge.

I am interested in politicians as an institution, and I like them as people. I devote countless hours to talking to them. On the basis of these talks, as well as through reading and general observation, I find prayers and tears *and* presents are likely to be associated together. There is this difference, however. Whereas the people may applaud the recognition of the first two, they condemn the public official who accepts gifts. And yet in applauding the man who is moved by tears, they are doing their utmost to prepare him to be swayed by presents. The nature of the democratic process is such that our representatives are most strongly urged—and sometimes by the clergy—to bend the law to favor a particular individual. The favoritism shown the guilty may be hailed in certain quarters as the mark of magnanimity—but the poor widow-mother argument may be an enemy of justice.

The matter may not be as simple as it looks here, of

course. One might argue that love is greater than the law and base his argument on the thirteenth chapter of I Corinthians. Jesus Christ was interested in mercy as well as justice. The question then arises: Love for whom? If one's loyalty is to love in the biblical sense there are still the rights or values of society to be considered as well as those of the lone individual who has been trapped. I cannot speak of all cases, but I find that judges that depart from the law because of some higher justice are the ones most likely to get around the law for some inferior reason too.

What holds for local politicians holds for legislators too. Lincoln was not the first executive to know that legislators who cannot be moved by prayers may be swayed by jobs. "Lincoln was a supreme politician. He understood politics because he understood human nature." C. A. Dana, the Secretary of War, said that he "had an illustration of this in the spring of 1864." Lincoln believed that if he could get the constitution amended to prohibit slavery it would be worth at least a million men to the North. To do this required the support of three-fourths of the states. The State of Nevada was organized for that purpose. The question of admitting Nevada into the Union was to be decided by Congress. Lincoln felt that the vote was too close. He asked Dana to line up three congressmen—one from New Jersey, two from New York.

"What will they be likely to want?" Dana asked. "I don't know," said the President. "I don't know. It makes no difference, though, what they want. Here is the alternative: that we carry this vote, or be compelled to raise another million, and I don't know how many more, men, and fight no one knows how long. It is a question of three votes or new armies."

Dana sent for the three congressmen and saw them separately. Two wanted internal revenue collectors' appointments. The other wanted an important customs house appointment that paid about $20,000 a year.

The men got the jobs, Lincoln got their votes, and the United States got peace that much sooner, and how many lives were saved no one can tell. But lives were saved.[7]

One reacts violently against men who must be bought, especially in time of war, to do their duty. Lincoln seems none the less great for having bought the legislators' votes with jobs. In doing this he demonstrates his loyalty to a paramount good—the lives of his people. If Lincoln stated the alternatives correctly, even the secretary of the National Civil Service Reform League must agree that a man is more precious than a job, and a million men and much else are worth more than three jobs. It is one of democracy's ways of meeting an emergency. As I think G. B. S. once pointed out, life is more than a gymnasium in which to exercise moral principles. Democracy's way, although imperfect, is probably incontestably better than death by violence for those who fail to see the light.

But if Lincoln's action was justified by the great emergency and the imperfect nature of man, what can be said for later presidents, governors, and other administrative officials who gave and do give jobs in peacetime to secure a desired bit of legislation. It is interesting to observe in Everystate, that governors, regardless of party, appoint cooperative legislators in the midst of their term to administrative positions. It is done without regard to party lines. It is a straw in the wind indicating that on one or more pieces of legislation the member's desire to get a job (or jobs) determined his vote.

Here the question is: Can any legislative program be so important to society that the executive is acting in the public interest when he persuades senators and assemblymen to vote for it, by giving them one or more jobs? The answer to this question is not easy, but it is easy to see that the legislator who will give his job for a vote places himself in an untenable position. But it is done, and logrolling is done, even in Everystate—"I will vote for your bill, if you will vote for mine"—although the law there has clearly spoken out against both of these practices.

One senator who has the habit of voting on the merits of the question said that he was penalized for so doing. "Commissioner X gave out fourteen jobs to get a larger appropriation for his commission. He gave a Senator's wife and two of her relatives jobs for his vote. Of course he gave me nothing because he knew that I would vote that way anyway."

These illustrations, or a thousand other similar ones, would not be interesting if they were not descriptive of one basic method followed by all kinds of executives in putting across a legislative program. Legislators who will not take cash for their vote may barter it for a job. The law may condemn both practices, but our public morality lags behind on the job bribe. It reminds one of Congressman T. V. Smith's statement that constituents who ask him to give some incompetent relative a job would not ask or expect him to dip his hand into the public treasury and give the incompetent relative a cash hand-out.

The findings of Samuel Seabury in New York were colossal in their magnitude. One public official deposited $520,000 in six years, of which $50,000 was his salary. Judge Olvany's sale of his political influence between the time he became leader of Tammany Hall and November 5, 1931, is indicated by the fact that his law firm deposited more than $5,280,000 which was not deposited in the firm's accounts. While he was a cabinet officer, Albert Fall had a black bag with $100,000 in it for a piece of our public domain. Jimmy Hines sold his political influence as a district leader to known gangsters, and once introduced District Attorney Dodge of New York City to one of these criminals and told the district attorney that these are the boys that put up the campaign fund money "to elect you." At another time Mr. Hines described Mr. Dodge as "stupid, respectable, and my man."

But I am not especially concerned with these people, because they are not the norm; they are not representative of the American politician or the American people. They have fallen and belong to our criminal class. But I am concerned with politicians in good standing in their respective communities, playing the game as they normally play it. For example, here is the case of a councilman who has forty years of public service behind him. He has weathered the depression in a great city. In 1937 the going was very rough. He took the money around to all the polling places in his district himself—money to be used in buying election officials and voters. "He didn't trust nobody." He got elected! A year later he was the chairman of a commission that had dealings with a great utility. The councilman was interested in helping an attorney with a job, but he had no job to give. He told the attorney to go to Mr. Bond, the head legal counsel, and say that Councilman X had sent him, and that he would like an appointment to the legal staff of the utility. He went and was offered a very minor position which he did not accept. A week later the eminent utility attorney called on the councilman to see about a hearing in which the utility was interested. The council-man was not sure when he could get his committee to-gether. The utility lawyer said that the matter was urgent. The councilman said that he was seriously interested in having Attorney P placed in a good position too, but sometimes it takes longer to work these things out than one would expect. The utility lawyer said, "Tell your man to come back, I will talk to him again." Attorney P called, was given a $3,800 job, the councilman immediately called his committee together for the hearing, the utility got a decision it could accept, and the episode was closed for everybody except the city—the problem of utility regu-lation is always before it.

These illustrations may well stand for ten thousand com-parable ones; they are not unique. They have their coun-terparts, at some time or other, in every county in the land. These are some of the ways that business is done by those who devote themselves to the people's business.

Last winter a state senator called on me at my apartment. He impressed me as being the kind of public official who votes on the merit of a question. He is interested in issues. I so appreciated our talk that I asked if he would have a drink of Scotch. He accepted and as he drank the amber-hued liquid, he said, "This stuff is easier for me to get in Crystal City than water." I was annoyed. I remarked that that was Ballantine's. He said it didn't matter, "It all comes free to me." I thought that if whiskey came free to him and his party, it must come very free to the others. He assured me that it did.

This comment might be used to introduce a discussion of lobbyists and pressure groups—they have a place in our pattern of politics—but so much has been written about them and their methods that I will make but one or two general observations. The legislator, whether national, state, or local, is a fallible individual like the rest of us. When he is asked to vote on a certain piece of legislation, particularly if it engages the attention of powerful or numerous individuals, he becomes the target of experts who begin to work on him. The methods of these individuals follow one or more of three general plans of attack. The lobbyist may attempt to convincingly show the merit or evil of the legislation under consideration. This service may be of distinct public value. A legislator cannot know everything about all legislative bills. The lobbyist may attempt to prove that the senator's constituents are strongly for or against the bill. Or the group that the lobbyist represents is very much interested in it, and should the member vote wrong, he could not hope to be returned. Or he might, by voting right, be promoted to higher honors. Garner is quoted as having said that he voted on measures according to principle, unless he found that two-thirds of the Democrats felt differently, and then he stood by his constituents. The third idea is to have as lobbyist a person who can call the legislator by his first name—a fellow with a flair for politicians. Then he gives the smile and the cordial greeting, and maybe a dinner, or whiskey or whatever it is that the legislator wants. The old primordial female argument is not unknown, neither is it as common as hotel bills paid, card games won, unnaturally large fees for services or merchandise sold to the lobbyists.

Finally, there is the bribe direct. The legislature has been strongly urged by one group of stores in Everystate to forbid merchants to give sales stamps when cash purchases are made. Another group of stores urged that this bill be defeated. Some observers have estimated that interested parties spent $50,000 on this legislation. One prominent senator said that the stamp bill was the most important piece of legislation that would ever come up in his lifetime. Other observers have estimated that from $30,000 to $50,000 was spent in that legislative battle. A man who knows some of the inner facts said $60,000 was spent. An assemblyman was taken over to the police station one night because he was drunk. When he was searched the officer found $1,400, and the fact that they had pulled in a legislator. They let him go, and said that he should have told them he was a member of the assembly. He said that he didn't mind, and when the officers looked at his money, he exclaimed it was nothing. "Why, some of the fellows got $2,600 for theirs." As Thoreau once remarked, "Some circumstantial evidence is very strong, as when you find a trout in the milk." A senator told me that he was offered $1,800 for his vote on this stamp bill, and although he never considered taking the money, the offer caused him some unhappy moments, for he could not decide how to vote on this measure, anyway. He could not tell where the interest of Everystate lay. He could not vote his convictions, because he had none. He could not take the money, but the bribe offer annoyed him in a way that he could not have foreseen.

This senator's testimony is valuable here, because his reaction to a bribe offer is more descriptive of the generality of public officials in Everystate than is the attitude of the few state legislators who may sell their vote. People may not change, but human relationships do. Politics has changed little in 2,000 years, but where there is free gov-

ernment today, the conditions of political life for the average man have improved. This is necessarily true of ethical
standards, practices, and attitudes. The first Republican
administration of Wisconsin, just before the Civil War,
was bought for half a million dollars by a railroad seeking land grants.

"The report discloses that many of the most prominent
leaders in the political life of the State had been corrupted
by the lobbyists, and that the railroad company had been
'guilty of numerous and unparalleled acts of mismanage-
ment, gross violation of duty, fraud and plunder.' Stocks
and Bonds of the company aggregating $175,000 had been
distributed among thirteen senators, and $355,000 in like
securities had been shared among thirty-nine members of
the assembly. The sum of $30,000 was divided equally
among three state officials, and $50,000 in bonds were de-
livered to Governor Bashford, after the signing of the
legislative grant, as a gratuity, to 'propitiate' his feelings." [8]

That corruption is a matter of time and circumstance
rather than a party matter is evident to anyone who reads
history. William A. Barstow, Democratic nominee for
governor in 1856, was first declared elected, and then un-
seated because of fraud. Many other states were vulnerable about this time too. It was a time of great change and
vast natural resources were being exploited; it was a day
when many individuals were "rugged" and ruthless. It was
part of a feudal period that America passed through in
coming of age. And that period is so recent that it is still
upon us in much the same way that the light of the setting
sun can be seen after the sun has disappeared beyond the
horizon's rim. Today, however, there are no free railroad
passes, and if a legislator tells the hotel waiter that his

bill is to be paid by a railroad or any other lobbyist, the item is worth a headline or an editorial in the Madison newspapers.

I think that there is an improvement in public morality all along the line. Organized crime has increased, perhaps; but nevertheless the general level of political life is higher than it has been at any time since the administration of Andrew Jackson.

Either, as I say, organized crime has increased or investigations, prosecutions, and convictions have increased. By organized crime I do not mean monopolies, or sporadic acts of violence by such groups as the Ku Klux Klan. I am thinking of crime as organized when criminals and public officials combine to supply goods or services that the law prohibits. Gambling, prostitution, liquor, rackets of various sorts come first to mind (and in 1940 an organized murder syndicate was discovered in New York City). So whether greater or not, crime is organized in different areas for the same general reasons that have led business and sales forces the country over to improve their organization in recent years. We Americans have a flair for organization, be it in finance, religion, politics, or crime. This genius for organization is one part of the story, and the background supporting this anti-social condition has been referred to—the fluidity of life, human wants that conflict with legal rights, the demand for personal freedom, the presence of the motor car, the failure of law-enforcing agencies, newspapers, and civic groups to uphold the law, and a curious attitude of mind that works to get a law passed, but does not work to enforce it.

The testimony taken at the trial of James Hines is a case in point. There one found that gangsters bought protection from a political leader who in turn was able to grant them immunity from the district attorney, the police, and the magistrates. This is the standard pattern. It is by no means limited to the big cities. Tom Rooski was a sheriff in a rural county of a semi-rural state. A slot machine gang was so powerful there that the sheriff not only permitted them to operate, contrary to the law, but he repaired the slot machines after they had broken down.

Last Thanksgiving I was invited to a dinner in a distant city. A police chief and his wife from a small town were also guests at the dinner. Trying to make conversation, I said to the chief, "How is the number racket in your town?" He replied "Fine." And then his wife spoke up and said, "You ought to know what happened to me. A fortune teller told me to play 848 and she said to play it for six weeks. I told the grocer that I wanted to box it, and I boxed it with two cents on each side, and then I boxed it with a nickel and then with a dime, and I played it for six weeks, but nothing happened. I told the grocer that I wasn't going to play it any more. He said that I should because he was sure that it was a good number. The next day I didn't play it, but the grocer played ten cents for me and ten cents for himself, but still nothing happened. The third day, he played ten cents for himself and nothing for me. And he won $50."

Two days later I was visiting at the home of a public official in a city of about 75,000. The story of the chief's wife had amused me, and I repeated it there. The public official said: "That's nothing. Our mayor controls the slot machines in our city, and he has put one son on the police force and another son in as city attorney. A tavern in the city had a number of slot machines from a competing company, and so the mayor's police drove up to the tavern, unloaded six of the mayor's slot machines, put them in, and carried away the slot machines that did not belong to the mayor. The head of the rival organization then got the constable that was not friendly to the mayor to deputize a number of men and to pick up about fifty of the mayor's slot machines. He picked them up, put them in an empty building, and had six of his constables stand guard. The mayor sent down a gang of men. They beat up the six constables, took the slot machines away, and that was that. The police on the corner continued to stand on the corner, and that was all.

"The constable then got ten of the mayor's new slot machines, took them to his home, had newspaper men come and take a picture of them as he was about to destroy them. He substituted ten old machines in place of the mayor's ten new ones and destroyed the old machines. That would have been all right, but a newspaper man took a picture of the machines actually destroyed, and there was some excitement."

If slot machines are found wherever people spend money, and if numbers are sold in drug stores, grocery stores, taverns, barber shops, and on the street, and if anyone able to walk can buy a number or pull a lever on the slot machine, one can assume that the police and the district attorney and the sheriff and probably the lower courts, and sometimes higher officials as well, are not representing the people but are probably being paid by organized crime. There are two alternatives before them: to change the law that makes gambling illegal or to enforce the law. To legalize gambling would not do away with organized crime, but it would in many areas go far to lessen the appeal of organized crime inasmuch as one of its strengths is the ability it has to satisfy wants that the law denies.

The situation in which public morality in this country has improved generally, and yet organized crime has increased, is not wholly unlike the situation in public health. Public health has improved enormously during the last few decades, but more people die of cancer today than in 1910 or before. Fortunately, we do know how to destroy organized crime; but the learned men in medicine know less about how to destroy cancer.

That public morality has generally improved can be discovered by talking to men in politics today who were active in politics thirty years or more ago. Just recently I found an item in the newspaper with a picture of an old, old man. He was in the news this one time because he had voted for President Lincoln twice in the same election. Of course, time is a solvent and may, in the minds of many people, wash away guilt. Col. John Alley has recently written about the beginnings of city government in Oklahoma territory. The pioneers had just moved in—the law lagged behind. They tried electing officers for the townsite of Guthrie by *viva voce*, but they got nowhere.

"A new method of balloting was devised. Three farm-wagons were drawn up in a row and the candidates each mounted a separate wagon. The voters then formed in three lines, each line passing the wagon of his favorite, and a teller for each counted heads as they passed. A novel form of 'ballot stuffing' soon became apparent. It was discovered that many voters, after passing the wagons, would return to the rear of the line and pass the teller for a second counting. Despairing of an equitable decision, the convention finally adjourned to meet at nine o'clock the following morning." [9]

Here the fluidity of life encouraged the disregard for legal forms. There were no legal forms in Guthrie in 1889 —there was no state. Congress had not legislated for this territory.

To cite the example of an old city. One day an Irishman in Philadelphia explained the way he stuffed ballot boxes as a young man (but he doesn't do it any more). He said, "I haven't crooked a vote for a long time." I thought he had had a change of heart. He said, "No, it's too dangerous now—the law—I wouldn't do it." A young university man was asked by a division leader to add 300 ballots to a box. He said, "I cannot do that, Mr. ———." He then explained to me that it was too dangerous, might change his whole future. He could not take that chance. I know that there are other election officials who still do take that chance, but there is something in the air today that wasn't there thirty or more years ago. And this something, plus more effective administrative and reform organizations, helps keep elections clean.

One time a father told his ten-year-old son that he should not play "war," but that he should play games of peace. The son asked, "Daddy, can you show us how to play 'peace'?" (War can more readily be dramatized, and graft lends itself to story telling.) But the truth is that in the United States peace and honesty are the general rule. If graft is not exactly the exception, yet it is a well-defined departure from the norm and it is restricted to a very small per cent of our voters and our politicians. The incorruptible legislator, and there are many of them, is celebrated for all time in *The Moral Discourses of Epictetus:*

"This Priscus Helvidius too saw, and acted accordingly: For when Vespasian had sent to forbid his going to the senate, he answered, 'It is in your power to prevent my continuing a senator; but while I am one, I must go.'—'Well then at least be silent there.'—'Do not ask my opinion, and I will be silent.'—'But I must ask it.'—'And I must speak what appears to me to be right.'—'But if you do, I will put you to death.'—'Did I ever tell you that I was immortal? You will do your part and I mine: It is yours to kill, and mine to die intrepid; yours to banish me, mine to depart untroubled.'

"What good, then, did Priscus do, who was but a single person? Why what good does the purple do to the garment? What but the being a shining character in himself, and setting a good example to others? Another, perhaps, if in such circumstances Caesar had forbidden his going to the senate, would have answered, 'I am obliged to you for excusing me.' But such a one he would not have forbidden to go, well knowing that he would either sit like a statue, or, if he spoke, he would say what he knew to be agreeable to Caesar, and would overdo it by adding still more." [10]

And then to come on to our own country, and at a time when Tweed was most powerful and most corrupt. George Jones, the proprietor of the *New York Times*, was offered $5,000,000 for his silence and he refused. Walpole's dictum that "Those men there have their price" may have been true of the men that Walpole knew, but it is not descriptive of all the politicians or all the voters in America. The Tweed Ring sent an influential banker to Thomas Nast. (Tweed has said that many of his people could not read, but they could see pictures.) The banker offered Nast $100,000 for "expenses" to study art in Europe. I quote Samuel P. Orth's account of the conversation.

" 'Do you think I could get $200,000?' innocently asked Nast.

" 'I believe from what I have heard in the bank that you might get it.'

"After some reflection, the cartoonist asked: 'Don't you think I could get $500,000 to make that trip?'

" 'You can; you can get $500,000 in gold to drop this Ring business and get out of the country.'

" 'Well, I don't think I'll do it,' laughed the artist. 'I made up my mind not long ago to put some of those fellows behind the bars, and I am going to put them there.'

" 'Only be careful, Mr. Nast, that you do not first put yourself in a coffin,' said the banker as he left." [11]

The brilliant Brand Whitlock so beautifully described a state legislator who could not be bought that I want to quote him rather fully:

"And yet there was beauty there in the state legislature, moral beauty, as there ever is somewhere in man. . . .

"The old Egyptian stood there while the long roll was being called, and the crisis approached and the nervous tension was a keen pain. And suddenly one of the gas lobbyists went up to him, there on the verge of the House, and began to talk with him. I had the story a good while afterwards from one of the whips, who, it seemed, knew all that had gone on that night. The lobbyist of course knew about the man, knew especially about his necessities, as lobbyists do; and he began to talk to the old fellow about them—about his poverty and his children, and he used the old argument which has been employed so long and so successfully with the rural members of our legislatures, and has been the source of so much evil in our city governments, that is, that the bill concerned only Chicago, and that the folks down home would neither know nor care how he voted on it, and then how much two thousand dollars would mean to him. As the lobbyist talked, there were various eyes that looked at him, waiting for a sign; they needed only a few votes then and the roll-call was being delayed by one pretense and another, and the clock on the wall, inexorably ticking toward the hour of that legislature's dissolution, was turned back. The old fellow listened and stroked his chin, and then presently when the lobbyist had done, he turned his old blue eyes on him and said:

" 'I reckon you're right: I'm poor, and I've got a big family. And you're right, too, when you say my people won't know nor care: they won't; they don't know nor care a damn; they won't send me back here of course. And God knows what's to come of my wife and my children; I am going home to them tomorrow and on Monday I'm going to hunt me a job in the harvest-field; I reckon I'll die in the poorhouse. Yes, I'm going home—but'—he stopped and looked the lobbyist in the eyes—'I'm going home an honest man.' " [12]

I cannot reduce all of my varied, and often conflicting ideas about the American voter to a single principle. Life is more than logic. We touch the extremes more often than the golden mean. We do not usually follow the Greek thinker who said, "Nothing in excess." We are better described by Pinckney's declaration: "Millions for defense, but not one cent for tribute." We are often rushing about immersed in our own affairs, but we can drop everything and spend billions for a noble cause. We are sometimes selfish about little things, but we can give in the grand manner. We live and let live, and the idea that we must now think about planning disturbs us. We are honest more often than not so far as personal relationships go, but we are not yet educated to treat corporations with this same quality of honesty. We sometimes mistake bigness for grandeur, newness for merit; we often try short cuts to culture; but we also spend a large portion of our income on education —education for everybody. We may pay lip service to ideals that we privately ignore. Many of us love humbugs but we uniformly hate chiselers and shysters. We doff our hats to the big crook—until he is convicted! We punish the man who steals bread more than the one who steals a railroad. We have youth, freedom, energy, great initiative in certain fields, and colossal faith—though just now questions are forming in our minds.

FOOTNOTES

[1] *The Autobiography of Lincoln Steffens*, p. 574. Harcourt, Brace and Company, publishers.

[2] *New York Herald Tribune*, June 14, 1901.

[3] The Intermediate Report of Samuel Seabury to the Hon. Samuel H. Hofstadter Committee, dated January 25, 1932, contains a mine of pertinent and detailed information on the manner in which certain public officials in New York City carved up the public's apple there and sold it to private interests. Also see the valuable discussions of this material in J. B. Northrop and W. B. Northrop, *The Insolence of Office*, and in Norman Thomas and Paul Blanshard, *What's the Matter with New York?*

[4] *Ibid.*

[5] *The Autobiography of Lincoln Steffens*, pp. 527-528. Harcourt, Brace and Company, publishers.

[6] *Autobiography* by Robert M. La Follette, p. 67.

[7] C. A. Dana, *Recollections of the Civil War*, pp. 174-177. Cited in Charles A. Beard, *American Government and Politics*, pp. 214-216.

[8] *Badger Saints and Sinners*, by Fred L. Holmes, p. 160.

[9] *City Beginnings in Oklahoma Territory*, p. 19 (John Alley).

[10] *The Moral Discourses of Epictetus* (trans. by Elizabeth Carter), Chapter II.

[11] Samuel P. Orth, *The Boss and the Machine*, pp. 77-78.

[12] Brand Whitlock, *Forty Years of It*, pp. 98-100. D. Appleton-Century Company, publishers.

CHAPTER II
TALK VERSUS BULLETS

"In nothing are we more representative of our people than in this chronic taste for talk."—*Politics and Public Service* by Leonard D. White and T. V. Smith, p. 243.

The American politician is as modern as today's newspaper, yet he is older than the democracy of Pericles. He goes back to the earliest governments of primitive man. For there came a time when even primitive man could not rule by force alone; he had to use suasion too, and when you have suasion, you have the politician. The earliest long narrative that western civilization possesses about him is the story of David in the Bible—a story doubtless written by one in King David's court. And in this earliest of political narratives we already have a full-grown politician on his way to power.

Absalom was the son of King David, and Absalom wanted to be king. To win the attention of the people he arranged to have chariots and horses and fifty men run before him. He arose early and stood by the way of the gate leading into the city of the king. Absalom intercepted each man that came with a complaint and asked who he was, and what was wrong. He then explained that the man's cause was good and right, but, unfortunately, he could not get justice from the present king. But he added, "Oh, that I were made judge in the land, that every man which hath any suit or cause might come unto me, and I would do him justice," and he took into his arms and kissed those who came to do obeisance to him. "And on this manner did Absalom to all Israel that came to the king for judgment: *so Absalom stole the hearts of the men of Israel.*" [1]

From Absalom to Franklin Roosevelt, Arthur Vandenberg, and Paul V. McNutt is a long time in the recorded history of man, but as we examine the record, and particularly the record of Western man in eras of peace, we are bound to be impressed with the sovereign power of human speech, as Absalom and his successors have used it. Medieval philosophers were not unique in thinking that speech was the divine in man—the God-given attribute that sets man off from and above the rest of the animal world. Man cannot run as the deer, or see as the eagle, or lift as the elephant, or fly as the swallow, or swim as the trout, yet he is master of the world because he can think and talk. There is no substitute for thought and talk—for thinking that is not articulate is valueless. The ability to talk, to talk to one man or to millions, is the attribute in man that most effectively distinguishes him from his fellows, and from other animals as well. And for those who talk well, it is the sure means to immortality. The words of Jesus are more powerful today than they were when Pontius Pilate asked, "What is Truth?" Shakespeare is alive wherever civilized men meet, or when they reflect on the nature of their pilgrimage through this world. Washington's, Jefferson's, or Lincoln's words weigh more heavily with untold millions of voters today than do the counsels of those whose names will appear on the ballots in November. It is safe to say that the art of governing, either in the days of the Caesars or in those of our contemporaries—Mussolini, Stalin, Hitler, Churchill, and Roosevelt—is largely based on talk, the ability to paint pictures with words, or the skill in fashioning symbols of love and hate.

Absalom lived about the year 1000 B.C. From a different quarter of the ancient world and about two hundred years later comes another picture of the talker; although it is shadowy as myth, yet it vividly depicts the value of speech or oratory (even in war time) as a persuader of men. Talk was most highly esteemed by the Greeks, and their leaders had golden tongues. Homer's *Iliad*, which is an artistic expression of the folk stories that stemmed from the long siege and capture of Troy, depicts the man of words. "Then in their midst rose up Nestor, pleasant of speech, the clear-voiced orator of the Pylians, he from whose tongue flowed discourse sweeter than honey." [2]

And then Nestor spoke to the Warriors so effectively that Agamemnon said, "Verily hast thou again outdone the sons of the Achaians in speech, old man. Ah, father Zeus and Athene and Apollo, would that among the Achaians I had ten such councillors; then would the city of King Priam soon bow beneath our hands, captive and wasted." [3]

Odysseus was another honey-tongued persuader of man. Right at a time when the Achaians were eager to abandon the city of Priam and return home they were addressed by Odysseus, and he completely won them to the further prosecution of the war. Homer has written, "So spake he, and the Argives shouted aloud, and all round the ships echoed terribly to the voice of the Achaians as they praised the saying of god-like Odysseus." [4]

*   *   *

One finds in taking a long look at the record of Man and his government that whether a people live under the tyrants of Greece and Sicily, or the dictators of Rome, Germany or Russia, there is no personal security where there is no freedom of discussion. Free speech is liberty's shadow; when it is gone, liberty has already disappeared. And when the liberty of the individual goes, other basic values, both tangible and intangible, like adequate food and ease of soul, go with it, until man is no longer a man—or even a mouse that has a sort of freedom—but an automaton. And this is why a mature citizen will give up much rather than lose his personal liberty, his freedom to think and talk as he will. The dictatorships that have come into power in the world today—before 1940—are in each and every case in a country whose people were politically immature to begin with, people who were not sufficiently experienced in the art of self-government—that is, government by public discussion—to manage their own affairs in times of stress and economic disaster. In countries like our own and England, the people have had a long experience with the democratic process; they know that there is only one alternative to a government by violence and that is a government by public discussion. So long as a people has the wit, imagination, and knowledge to talk about public affairs in times of stress it is most likely to remain free.

If President Roosevelt ordered the immediate execution of Al Smith, W. R. Hearst, and other critics of his administration, one would have a clear and vivid example of what happens when free speech is no more, and of what actually is happening under the dictators. Words often seem so futile, and public discussion may appear to be useless; yet the experience of the ages testifies that when talk about community problems is abandoned, free government cannot endure. If the individual citizen does not want a Hitler blood purge or the many executions that are given to critics of the Russian rule, or some of the lesser manifestations of autocratic government, he is bound to be actively and articulately concerned about politics, the politician, and public discussion.

Pericles expressed this idea in the fifth century before Christ. His funeral oration for those who had fallen in the Peloponnesian War compels our attention not only because of its wisdom but also because Pericles was the statesman who administered the public affairs of Athens at the summit of her power and glory. He said in part:

"Our public men have, besides politics, their private affairs to attend to, and our ordinary citizens, though occupied with the pursuits of industry, are still fair judges of public matters; for, unlike any other nation, *regarding him who takes no part in these duties not as unambitious but as useless, we Athenians are able to judge at all events if we cannot originate, and instead of looking on discussion as a stumbling-block in the way of action, we think it an indispensable preliminary to any wise action at all.*" [5]

A few years ago another leader, Henry A. Wallace, urged the need for public discussion in deciding which of three paths—internationalism, nationalism, or a planned middle course—America shall take. He says that first of all we must decide which way we want to go. Regardless of the course chosen, it must have the understanding allegiance of the people. This in turn requires "time and literally hundreds of millions of personal contacts as the educational or propaganda process is carried out." [6] "That question should be debated throughout America, and on the highest possible plane. It should be debated in Congress, in public forums, in city and in country schoolhouse meetings in every state. This time, our course must not be decided behind closed doors, either in Washington or on Wall Street. The people must be let in on the problem. This time, let us open the doors and debate our future course throughout the length and breadth of the land." [7]

Democracy is government by public discussion; and it was easier to manage in the small city states of Pericles' Greece or in the town meetings of New England in the days of Samuel Adams, when the world that touched the voter was comparatively small and the individual knew his neighbors. Man lived in a self-contained community and he was familiar with his environment. Furthermore, the tasks of governments were few, and there was some merit in the argument of Andrew Jackson that a man was fit for any office that he could get. But the problem confronting those interested in democratic government today is enormously more difficult than it was when people lived in our earlier and simpler communities. A few thousand people living in a small area form a community in which the citizens can know one another, their politicians, and what the government is or is not doing; but when several thousand or several million people live in the small area called a city it is no longer a community, and often not even a collection of communities; instead it is an aggregation of individuals. Here as Walter Lippmann says, "the real environment is altogether too big, too complex, and too fleeting for direct acquaintance." [8] Man cannot know his politicians, or what his government is doing, without real effort on his part to find out the facts. This is why popular government must be supported by popular information.

Woodrow Wilson indicated his belief in the value of talk, and talk about public affairs, when he wrote, "I conceive it to be one of the needs of the hour to restore the processes of common counsel. We must learn, we freemen, to meet as our fathers did, somehow, somewhere, for consultation. There must be discussion . . . in which all freely partici-pate." [9]

Along with this change in size of the world in which democratic man lives, there is an equally great change in the nature of his government. The idea that that govern-ment is best that governs least has been abandoned for the idea that the best government is the one that is most useful to the people. The social service state has taken the place of the police state. Government is so vital to the people to-day that for more than twenty millions of them it provides food, clothing, and shelter, and for even more millions its policies determine whether or not a man has a job, and the kind of job it is, the rate of pay, and the hours an individual must labor. It determines the number of acres a farmer plants and what he receives for his produce. In short, there is only one institution in our modern democratic society that touches the individual so intimately and so continu-ously as government, and that is the family.

Because government is so vital to our existence today the need for talk based on knowledge of public affairs is urgent. The Roosevelt administration, under the guidance of John W. Studebaker, United States Commissioner of Education, and in cooperation with the public school sys-tems, has established some hundreds of public forums. These forums involve an attendance of thousands of citi-zens led by trained educators. The forum means organized public discussion by a regularly scheduled assemblage of citizens, a capable leader, a real problem for discussion. It is an expression of the people's growing awareness of their government; millions are government-conscious today who never before gave it a thought. And yet even today the number of citizens that critically and constructively examine and discuss government, that is, the politician and his policies, is only a fraction of the more than 75,000,000 adults in the United States.

The forum movement helps create for citizens in a democracy what Norman Angell has called a grammar of truth. He has brilliantly written about our need for this grammar of truth as well as a grammar of language in order to increase the political literacy of the voter. This grammar of evidence or of truth means the development of a sort of aptitude that will help citizens "in the interpretation of those things, we are compelled to judge every day in our ordinary lives."

"I suggested that no apparatus could give the ordinary man sufficient control over his government to constitute democracy unless at least he knows what he wants, is able to 'judge general results,' simple everyday social and political phenomena that touch him in his daily life, with some correctness, is able to distinguish broadly between what he can and can not know (as that he can know whether his water is polluted and his taxes going up, but cannot know which of ten candidates would make the best city engineer)." [10]

Commissioner Studebaker is by no means alone in thinking that this central faculty of judging "general results" can best be fostered by regular and systematic organized public discussion. He concludes his timely book on the subject with the following paragraph:

"Frequently when I propose the extension of adult civic education through public affairs forums, I am faced with this retort: 'Do you think we can talk our way out of our difficulties?' This remark is usually followed by an appeal for action. Let me leave you with this thought. Democracy means action by the majority. Therefore, no vital problem can be solved the democratic way until the majority of people understand its solution. Anybody who wants to get to solutions without the understanding and intelligent support of the majority is simply not a believer in democracy. I am a believer in democracy. I am willing to wait for solutions until the majority is intelligent enough to support them. But, I know that if the masses of the people do not discuss and talk about their problems constantly, real solutions will not be solved by the democratic technique. Eventually, democracy will go down, collapse because of its inability to meet real problems. For that reason I advocate with all my energy the extension and improvement of the means of mass education on public affairs. Intelligent action depends upon a *program of intelligent discussion*." [11]

Another significant expression of the forum idea is America's Town Meeting of the Air. Each week, the Town Hall, New York, in cooperation with the National Broadcasting Company, presents a vital and interesting subject for discussion by experts of varying opinions. Following a brief statement of opinion by each of the speakers, the audience present is urged to ask questions—and searching questions are asked. To mention a few of the recently discussed topics and their leaders will probably best describe this forum of the air.

How Can We Defend Democracy in America Now? Harold L. Ickes, Hugh S. Johnson, Mrs. Herbert H. Lehman.

Should the Arms Embargo Be Lifted? Frank Knox, Philip F. La Follette.

What Are the Real Issues in the European War? John Gunther, Anne O'Hare McCormick, Jay Allen.

How Will the War Situation Affect Unemployment? John Carmody, Mark Jones, Henry Pratt Fairchild.

Should We Ignore Racial Differences? Ernest A. Hooton, M. F. Ashley-Montague, Kirtley F. Mather.

What Does American Democracy Mean to Me? Pietro di Donato, H. Jerry Voorhis, E. McNeill Poteat, Mary McLeod Bethune, Alice Salomon, Jack McMichael, W. Selden Washington.

What Kind of Peace Can Europe Make? John Gunther, Maurice Hindus, Linda Littlejohn, Friedrich E. Auhagen.

Can Business and Government Work Together Today? Robert A. Taft, Jerome Frank, Floyd B. Odlum, William McC. Martin, Jr.

America and Japan—Embargo or New Treaty? Harry E. Yarnell, William R. Castle, Walter H. Judd.

What Can Americans Do for Humanity Today? Stanley High, Rufus M. Jones, Mabel T. Boardman, James G. McDonald.

Should We Continue to Restrict Agricultural Production? Ransom Aldrich, Robert B. Snowden, Jr.

Should the Dies Investigation Be Continued? S. B. Pettengill, R. N. Baldwin.

Should We Extend the Reciprocal Trade Act? H. F. Grady, L. J. Taber.

Does America Need Compulsory Health Insurance? Dr. Henry E. Sigerist, Dr. Terry M. Townsend, Dr. C. E. A. Winslow.

Should We Stay in the Philippines? Paul V. McNutt, Nicholas Roosevelt, Raymond Leslie Buell.

Employers, Employees, and the Public. H. L. Nunn, E. Keating, A. E. Roth.

Should Controversial Subjects Be Discussed in Schools? John W. Studebaker, C. Harold Caulfield, Alice Keliher.

How Can Philosophy and Religion Meet Today's Needs? Irwin Edman, Harry A. Overstreet, Frank Kingdon, Father Martin C. D'Arcy.

What Should Government Spend for—Armaments, Agriculture, Relief, Construction? A. A. Ballantine, Elmo Roper, H. S. Dennison, J. B. Carey.

Are We on the Road to War? Frederick L. Schuman, César Saerchinger, Norman Thomas, James G. McDonald.

Are We Americans Basically a Moral People? Margaret Culkin Banning, Lewis Browne, Chester A. Creider, Kirtley F. Mather.

What Are the Essential Differences Between the Republican and the Democratic Parties? Robert H. Jackson, Glenn Frank.

The following description of the Town Meeting idea is found in the printed pamphlet of each broadcast. Since it has great informational value, I quote it here:

"One of the first acts of American colonists was to build a 'meeting house' in which every citizen had a voice in his government—a force for political education and action.

"During the spring of 1935 the town-meeting idea was adapted to the radio in an experimental series broadcast in cooperation with the NATIONAL BROADCASTING COMPANY from the TOWN HALL, New York. Almost immediately the program achieved nationwide popularity. Now in its fifth season, 'America's Town Meeting of the Air,' broadcast on Thursday evenings from 9:30 to 10:30, E.S.T., over the NBC Blue Network, is recognized as the nation's authoritative forum for the discussion of public questions." [12]

*   *   *

Whether or not a city has an established forum, it is sure to have one standard institution for stimulating thought and discussion among voters. I refer to the politicians. And while forums help educate thousands of citizens, the politicians catch the attention of millions. One of the chief reasons why the politician is indispensable in our democracy is that he keeps voters awake—or at least he does more than anyone else, or any other agency, to keep them awake, year in and year out, in every county, town, and precinct, telling them what the score is, making the issues and the problems of the great society meaningful to them. This is his business.

How well he does it depends upon the voters themselves. He is like the rest of us; he does what he must. His educational work is posited on the fundamental law that the limit of attention is not only the limit of democracy but the limit of the candidate's votes. *The politician is a vote-getter.* If to get votes he must discuss issues, he necessarily discusses issues, as politicians do in the politically mature community of Wisconsin. But if Big Bill Thompson thinks that a girl show or a cowboy lashing a long leather thong around the ample throat of a cowgirl will best win his citizens' attention in Chicago, then he will give them that. (In 1931 in Big Bill Thompson's last campaign for Mayor, I was one of several thousand present at a Thompson political meeting. As an entertainer was doing a particularly Minsky-like dance, I heard a man near me say, "God, I will vote for Bill Thompson as long as I live." The political maturity of this remark is nil. It is descriptive of Chicago in that a candidate for a major office in a politically mature community would not have used appeals of this sort for gaining support at the polls.)

The older La Follette for long months at a time worked eighteen hours a day on this problem of educating the voters. His testimony is common in the annals of politics. "I spoke forty-eight days in succession, never missing one single day, excepting Sundays. I averaged eight and one-quarter hours a day on the platform. We had two automobiles, so that if one broke down or got out of order in any way, I could transfer to the other." [13] He was realistic enough to know that he could not serve the people without having their attention and understanding of what he was doing. He wrote:

"I thought it all over. It was clear to me that the only way to beat boss and ring rule was to keep the people thoroughly informed. Machine control is based upon misrepresentation and ignorance. Democracy is based upon knowledge. It is of first importance that the people shall know about their government and the work of their public servants. 'Ye shall know the truth, and the truth shall make you free.' This I have always believed vital to self-government.

"Immediately following my election to Congress I worked out a complete plan for keeping my constituents informed on public issues and the record of my services in Congress; it is the system I have used in constantly widening circles ever since. . . .[14]

"When some Congressman made a speech on sound money—Reed or Carlisle—I would get the necessary number of copies of that speech, and send them to those interested in the money question. When the Oleomargarine bill, the Interstate Commerce bill, and other important legislation was pending, I sent out speeches covering the debates thoroughly. In this way I suppose I sent out hundreds of thousands of speeches, my own and others. . . .[15]

"The task of building up and maintaining an intelligent interest in public affairs in my district and afterward in the state, was no easy one. But it was the only way for me, and I am still convinced that it is the best way." [16]

In 1928, when Franklin Roosevelt nominated Al Smith for the presidency, he asked the rhetorical question, "What sort of president do we need today?" He answered his query by saying it should be a man who has four great qualifications, and among these four: "and in this time, most vital, that rare ability to make popular government function as it was intended to by the fathers, to reverse the present trend towards apathy, and arouse in the citizenship an active interest—a willingness to reassume its share of responsibility for the nation's progress. So only can we have, once more, a government not just for the people, but by the people also."

Not Al Smith, but Roosevelt himself best demonstrates his claim to his high office on this score of making the public government-conscious. No president during the lifetime of any voter now living has so consistently and indefatigably, in season and out, talked to the people about their government and what it is doing for them. His fireside talks have done more than a thousand textbooks to make the people think about their part in our democratic system. Voters of whatever faith, and whether or not they sit up and pay attention to the President, are at least reminded, when they are addressed in the following fashion, that they are voters—rulers in our democracy, the most indispensable part of our democratic process.

"Our government, happily, is a democracy. As a part of the democratic process your president is again taking an opportunity to report on the progress of national affairs to the real rulers of this country—the voting public." [17] Later in another fireside chat to the nation, Roosevelt, as pedagogue, continued his instructions.

"It is my hope that everybody affiliated with any party will vote in the primaries, and that every such voter will consider the fundamental principles for which his party is on record. That makes for a healthy choice between the candidates of the opposing parties on election day in November. . . . As the head of the Democratic party, however, charged with the responsibility of carrying out the definitely liberal declaration of principles set forth in the 1936 Democratic platform, I feel that I have every right to speak in those few instances where there may be a clear issue between candidates for a Democratic nomination involving these principles or involving a clear misuse of my name. . . . And I am concerned about the attitude of a candidate or his sponsors with respect to the rights of American citizens to assemble peaceably and to express publicly their views and opinions on important social and economic issues. I hope the liberal candidates will confine themselves to argument and not resort to blows. In nine cases out of ten the speaker or writer who, seeking to influence public opinion, descends from calm argument to unfair blows hurts himself more than his opponent.

"The Chinese have a story on this—a story based on three or four thousand years of civilization: Two Chinese coolies were arguing heatedly in the midst of a crowd. A stranger expressed surprise that no blows were being struck. His Chinese friend replied, 'The man who strikes first admits that his ideas have given out.'

"I know that neither in the summer primaries nor in the November elections will the American voters fail to spot the candidate whose ideas have given out."

Bruce Barton, though a Republican congressman, made very much the same point the next day, in describing the weakness of the Republican party, on one hand, and the contribution of the Roosevelt Democracy, on the other, in reminding the people of their place in our government.

"We spoke patronizingly of politics and politicians. We fell into the ghastly error of assuming that democracy is an easy form of government, whereas it is of all forms the hardest to preserve and make work.

"I say that my generation forgot how to work. And I say another thing—we lost our touch with common men and women. The strength of the New Deal is more than a willingness to work. Its strength is that it thinks and talks always of people.

"We Republicans used to be close to the people. Our party was founded as a people's party. Abraham Lincoln and his associates were of and for the people." [18]

If man is not wise enough to be governed by free discussion, then he is governed by force and bullets. The world spectacle in 1940 is telling proof on this point. The fact that it was always thus can be seen by reading the permanent observation of Machiavelli. He, who lived during the Renaissance in Italy, gives us an immortal picture of the politician, this time a man of force and tactics; but even here words are important because the people can better hear what the Prince says than see what he actually does.

Although the conditions of which he wrote and the art of governing then had more to do with bayonets than with ballots, yet many of his comments about men and their motives in public life are interesting to us now.

This man, who wrote *The Prince* in 1513, is the father of modern political science. He is the first one to see that no amount of "ought-ness" can ever equal a tiny fraction of "is-ness." He was employed by the state in different capacities. As Secretary of the Ten, he had gone on many ambassadorial missions, but he is important today because he had a seeing eye, a clear intellect, and was placed where he could view politics in a realistic fashion; he wrote only about men and their tactics as he saw them; and he rigorously followed an inductive psychological method. He had personal integrity, but he gave no more thought to morals than would a lecturer on termites or bacteria in the scientist's laboratory. He wanted to show how a strong and wise prince might turn events to his best advantage in first attaining control of and then ruling Italy. The four centuries that have passed since he wrote basically reaffirm his political astuteness.

First of all I quote from the eighteenth chapter in *The Prince*, "Concerning the Way in Which Princes Should Keep Faith," the chapter that has drawn the most fire from Machiavelli's critics.

"Every one admits how praiseworthy it is in a prince to keep faith, and to live with integrity and not with craft. Nevertheless our experience has been that those princes who have done great things have held good faith of little account, and in the end have overcome those who have relied on their word. You must know there are two ways of contesting, the one by the law, the other by force; the first method is proper to men, the second to beasts; but because the first is frequently not sufficient, it is necessary to have recourse to the second. . . . A prince, therefore, being compelled knowingly to adopt the beast, ought to choose the fox and the lion; because the lion cannot defend himself against snares and the fox cannot defend himself against wolves. Therefore, it is necessary to be a fox to discover the snares and a lion to terrify the wolves. Those who rely simply on the lion do not understand what they are about. Therefore a wise lord cannot, nor ought he to, keep faith when such observance may be turned against him, and when the reasons that caused him to pledge it exist no longer. If men were entirely good this precept would not hold, but because they are bad, and will not keep faith with you, you too are not bound to observe it with them. Nor will there ever be wanting to a prince legitimate reasons to excuse this non-observance. Of this endless modern examples could be given, showing how many treaties and engagements have been made void and of no effect through the faithlessness of princes; and he who has known best how to employ the fox has succeeded best.

"But it is necessary to know well how to disguise this characteristic, and to be a great pretender and dissembler; and men are so simple and so subject to present necessities, that he who seeks to deceive will always find some one who will allow himself to be deceived. One recent example I cannot pass over in silence. Alexander the Sixth did nothing else but deceive men, nor ever thought of doing otherwise, and he always found victims; for there never was a man who had greater power in asserting, or who with greater oaths would affirm a thing, yet would observe it less; nevertheless his deceits always succeeded according to his wishes, because he well understood this side of man-kind.

"Therefore it is unnecessary for a prince to have all the good qualities I have enumerated, but it is very necessary to appear to have them. And I shall dare to say this also, that to have them and always to observe them is injurious, and that to appear to have them is useful; to appear merci-ful, faithful, humane, religious, upright, and to be so, but with a mind so framed that should you require not to be so, you may be able and know how to change to the opposite.

"And you have to understand this, that a prince, espe-cially a new one, cannot observe all those things for which men are esteemed, being often forced, in order to main-tain the state, to act contrary to fidelity, friendship, hu-manity, and religion. Therefore it is necessary for him to have a mind ready to turn itself accordingly as the winds and variations of fortune force it, yet, as I have said above, not to diverge from the good if he can avoid doing so, but, if compelled, then to know how to set about it.

"For this reason a prince ought to take care that he never lets anything slip from his lips that is not replete with the above-named five qualities, that he may appear to him who sees and hears him altogether merciful, faithful, humane, upright, and religious. There is nothing more necessary to appear to have than this last quality, inasmuch as men judge generally more by the eye than by the hand, because it belongs to everybody to see you, to few to come in touch with you. Every one sees what you appear to be, few really know what you are, and those few dare not oppose themselves to the opinion of the many, who have the majesty of the state to defend them; and in the actions of all men, and especially of princes, which it is not prudent to challenge, one judges by the results.

"For that reason, let a prince have the credit of conquering and holding his state, the means will always be considered honest, and he will be praised by everybody; because the vulgar are always taken by what a thing seems to be and by what comes of it; and in the world there are only the vulgar, for the few find a place there only when the many have no ground to rest on.

"One prince of the present time, whom it is not well to name, never preaches anything else but peace and good faith, and to both he is most hostile, and either, if he had kept it, would have deprived him of reputation and kingdom many a time. . . .[19]

"Upon this question arises: whether it be better to be loved than feared or feared than loved? It may be answered that one should wish to be both, but, because it is difficult to unite them in one person, it is much safer to be feared than loved, when, of the two, either must be dispensed with. Because this is to be asserted in general of men, that they are ungrateful, fickle, false, cowards, covetous, and as long as you succeed they are yours entirely; they will offer you their blood, property, life, and children, as is said above, when the need is far distant; but when it approaches they turn against you. And that prince who, relying entirely on their promises, has neglected other precautions, is ruined, because friendships that are obtained by payments, and not by greatness or nobility of mind, may indeed be earned, but they are not secured, and in time of need cannot be relied upon; and men have less scruple in offending one who is beloved than one who is feared, for love is preserved by the link of obligation which, owing to the baseness of men, is broken at every opportunity for their advantage; but fear preserves you by a dread of punishment which never fails." [20]

*   *   *

Machiavelli wrote because he wanted men to act. Shakespeare had no ulterior motives and no master plan; he was the dramatist and poet, pure and undefiled. He held "the mirror up to nature"—save that he wrote in blank verse and his characters in his histories speak with the tongues of angels and archangels, not as kings and courtiers and servants speak in the flesh. Yet Shakespeare described the times and manners of his age; and his remarks about the politician sound familiar to the voters of 1940.

King Richard's statement to one of his companions, about Bolingbroke's attempt to woo the people, is descriptive of men seeking public office today:

> He is our cousin, cousin; but 'tis doubt,
> When time shall call him home from banishment,
> Whether our kinsman come to see his friends.
> Ourself and Bushy, Bagot here and Green
> Observ'd his courtship to the common people,
> How he did seem to dive into their hearts
> With humble and familiar courtesy,
> What reverence he did throw away on slaves,
> Wooing poor craftsmen with the craft of smiles
> And patient underbearing of his fortune,
> As 'twere to banish their affects with him.
> Off goes his bonnet to an oyster-wench;
> A brace of draymen bid God speed him well,
> And had the tribute of his supple knee,

With 'Thanks, my countrymen, my loving friends';
As were our England in reversion his,
And he our subjects' next degree in hope.[21]

In *King Lear* we find,

Get thee glass eyes;
And, like the scurvy politician seem
To see the things thou does not.[22]

We have the ominous comment from *Hamlet* that,

This might be the pate of a politician, . . . one that would
circumvent God, . . .[23]

The demagogue is portrayed so vividly and with such a
wealth of detail that one thinks of the promises of certain
American messiahs in our own depression era. Here, for
example, is Jack Cade, the rebel, speaking to the people
about the enormously "better times" that will be shared in
by all, but especially the poor, when he is made king. He
seems to use discussion, but actually he is attempting to gain
a vantage point where he can rely on force.

Be brave, then; for your captain is brave, and vows reforma-
tion. There shall be in England seven halfpenny loaves sold for
a penny; the three-hooped pot shall have ten hoops; and I will
make it felony to drink small beer. All the realm shall be in
common, and in Cheapside shall my palfrey go to grass. And
when I am king, as king I will be,—
    ALL: God save your majesty!
    CADE: I thank you, good people: there shall be no money; all
shall eat and drink on my score; and I will apparel them all in
one livery, that they may agree like brothers, and worship me
their lord.

DICK: The first thing we do, let's kill all the lawyers.

CADE: Nay, that I mean to do. Is not this a lamentable thing, that of the skin of an innocent lamb should be made parchment? that parchment, being scribbled o'er, should undo a man? Some say the bee stings; but I say, 'tis the bee's wax, for I did but seal once to a thing, and I was never mine own man since. How now! who's there? [24]

Again he appeals to the illiterate by ordering the hanging of the clerk of Chatham who can write.

CADE: I am sorry for 't: the man is a proper man of mine honour; unless I find him guilty, he shall not die. Come hither, sirrah, I must examine thee. What is thy name?

CLERK: Emmanuel.

DICK: They use to write it on the top of letters. 'Twill go hard with you.

CADE: Let me alone. Dost thou use to write thy name, or hast thou a mark to thyself, like an honest plain-dealing man?

CLERK: Sir, I thank God, I have been so well brought up, that I can write my name.

ALL: He hath confessed: away with him! he's a villain and a traitor.

CADE: Away with him! I say hang him with his pen and ink-horn about his neck.[25]

He is warned to flee before the forces of Sir Humphrey Stafford. He refuses and says that the knight will be encountered with a man as good as himself.

CADE: To equal him, I will make myself a knight presently. (Kneels) Rise up Sir John Mortimer. (Rises) Now have at him.[26]

After Jack Cade and his followers reached London he made another bid for the people's support.

Now is Mortimer lord of this city. And here, sitting upon London-stone, I charge and command that, of the city's cost, the pissing-conduit run nothing but claret wine this first year of our reign. And now, henceforward, it shall be treason for any that calls me other than Lord Mortimer.[27]

Before the Staffords were slain, Cade addressed his followers and summed up the cardinal point of his program in these words:

> And you, that love the commons, follow me.
> Now show yourselves men; 'tis for liberty.
> We will not leave one lord, one gentleman:
> Spare none but such as go in clouted shoon,
> For they are thrifty honest men, and such
> As would, but that they dare not, take our parts.[28]

The preceding passages from the writings of Machiavelli and Shakespeare on the power politician and the demagogue inevitably bring Hitler to mind. Fortunately for our purposes here, this leader has written that famous and strange volume, *Mein Kampf*—a combination of the beer-hall philosopher, the small grocer, and the mighty Wagner. I quote from this volume because it is descriptive of the technique, methods, and ideology of the leader of the German Reich— whose propaganda by talk has been his most influential ally, first in conquering the Germans, and then in conquering other peoples. Hitler, however, is different from the other authors I have quoted; probably this difference is best described by the following words from Edgar Ansell Mowrer: "Hitler cannot write. He makes speeches. He does not think. He gropes about until his mind hits a well-worn word-path and slides into an oration. His so-called ideas are canned formulae that hide wishes. They merely decorate his totally subjective ego. What he does know—how to lead men and women by the nose—is a matter of instinct. His book was written to strengthen his own belief in his mission."

Here follow a few of Hitler's reflections—an amorphous chaos of words and ideas. These I am quoting here deal with the power of the spoken word, and the nature of propaganda and the masses at whom it is directed.*

For let it be said to all knights of the pen and to all the political dandies, especially of today: the greatest changes in this world have never yet been brought about by a goose-quill!

No, the pen has always been reserved to motivate these changes theoretically.

But the power which set the greatest historical avalanches of political and religious nature sliding was, from the beginning of time, the magic force of the spoken word alone.

The great masses of a nation will always and only succumb to the force of the spoken word. But all great movements are movements of the people, are volcanic eruptions of human passions and spiritual sensations, stirred either by the cruel Goddess of Misery or by the torch of the word thrown into the masses, and are not the lemonade-like outpourings of aestheticizing *literati* and drawing-room heroes. [Page 136]

The psyche of the great masses is not receptive to half measures or weakness.

Like a woman, whose psychic feeling is influenced less by abstract reasoning than by an undefinable, sentimental longing for complementary strength, who will submit to the strong man rather than dominate the weakling, thus the masses love the ruler rather than the suppliant, and inwardly they are far

* Published by permission of and special arrangement with Houghton Mifflin Company, authorized publishers.

more satisfied by a doctrine which tolerates no rival than by the grant of liberal freedom; they often feel at a loss what to do with it, and even easily feel themselves deserted. They neither realize the impudence with which they are spiritually terrorized, nor the outrageous curtailment of their human liberties, for in no way does the delusion of this doctrine dawn on them. Thus they see only the inconsiderate force, the brutality and the aim of its manifestations to which they finally always submit. [Page 56]

By stamping Ludendorff as the culprit of the loss of the World War, one took away from the hand of the only dangerous accuser who was able to stand up against the traitors to the fatherland, the weapon of moral right. Therewith one started out with the very correct assumption that in the size of the lie there is always contained a certain factor of credibility, since the great masses of a people may be more corrupt in the bottom of their hearts than they will be consciously and intentionally bad, therefore with the primitive simplicity of their minds they will more easily fall victims to a great lie than to a small one, since they themselves perhaps also lie sometimes in little things, but would certainly still be too much ashamed of too great lies. Thus such an untruth will not at all enter their heads, and therefore they will be unable to believe in the possibility of the enormous impudence of the most infamous distortion in others; indeed, they may doubt and hesitate even when being enlightened, and they accept any cause at least as nevertheless being true; therefore, just for this reason some part of the most impudent lie will remain and stick; a fact which all great lying artists and societies of this world know only too well and therefore also villainously employ. [Pages 312-313]

All propaganda has to be popular and has to adapt its spiritual level to the perception of the least intelligent of those towards whom it intends to direct itself. Therefore its spiritual level has to be screwed the lower, the greater the mass of people which one wants to attract. But if the problem involved, like the propaganda for carrying on a war, is to include an entire people in its field of action, the caution in avoiding too high spiritual assumptions cannot be too great.

The more modest, then, its scientific ballast is, and the more it exclusively considers the feelings of the masses, the more striking will be its success. This, however, is the best proof whether a particular piece of propaganda is right or wrong, and not the successful satisfaction of a few scholars or "aesthetic" languishing monkeys.

This is just the art of propaganda that it, understanding the great masses' world of ideas and feelings, finds, by a correct psychological form, the way to the attention, and further to the heart, of the great masses. That our super-clever heads never understand this proves only their mental inertia or their conceit.

But if one understands the necessity of the attitude of the attracting skill of propaganda towards the great masses, the following rule then results:

It is wrong to wish to give propaganda the versatility of perhaps scientific teaching.

The great masses' receptive ability is only very limited, their understanding is small, but their forgetfulness is great. As a consequence of these facts, all effective propaganda has to limit itself only to a very few points and to use them like slogans until even the very last man is able to imagine what is intended by such a word. As soon as one sacrifices this basic principle and tries to become versatile, the effect will fritter away, as the masses are neither able to digest the material offered nor to retain it. Thus the result is weakened and finally eliminated. [Pages 232-234]

Exactly the same is the case with political advertising.

Propaganda's task is, for instance, not to evaluate the various rights, but far more to stress exclusively the one that is to be represented by it. It has not to search into truth as far as this is favorable to others, in order to present it then to the masses with doctrinary honesty, but it has rather to serve its own truth uninterruptedly.

It was fundamentally wrong to discuss the war guilt from the point of view that not Germany alone could be made responsible for the outbreak of this catastrophe, but it would have been far better to burden the enemy entirely with this guilt, even if this had not been in accordance with the real facts, as was indeed the case.

What, now, was the consequence of these half measures?

The great mass of a people is not composed of diplomats or even teachers of political law, nor even of purely reasonable individuals who are able to pass judgment, but of human beings who are as undecided as they are inclined towards doubts and uncertainty. As soon as by one's own propaganda even a glimpse of right on the other side is admitted, the cause for doubting one's own right is laid. The masses are not in a position to distinguish where the wrong of the others ends and their own begins. In this case they become uncertain and mistrusting, especially if the enemy does not produce the same nonsense, but, in turn, burdens their enemy with all and the whole guilt. What is more easily explained than that finally one's own people believe more in the enemy's propaganda, which proceeds more completely and more uniformly, than in one's own? This, however, may be said most easily of a people which suffers so severely from the mania of objectivity as the German people does. For now they will take pains not to do an injustice to the enemy, even at the risk of the severest strain on, or destruction of, his own nation and State.

But the masses do not at all realize that this is not the intention of the responsible authorities.

The people, in an overwhelming majority, are so feminine

in their nature and attitude that their activities and thoughts are motivated less by sober consideration than by feeling and sentiment. [Pages 236-237]

A change must never alter the content of what is being brought forth by propaganda, but in the end it always has to say the same. Thus the slogan has to be illuminated from various sides, but the end of every reflection has always and again to be the slogan itself. Only thus can and will propaganda have uniform and complete effect. [Page 239]

Talk is not everything to Hitler, but in the beginning there was talk. However, Der Fuehrer's talk would not have been enough had there not also been the Gestapo and a militaristic people, spiritually and physically terrorized. Furthermore, the kind of talk Hitler uses is as foreign to my idea of public discussion as would be the German's ubiquitous *Verboten* in an American community born and bred on the precept, "Express yourself."

Finally, before describing the American politician as he is today, I want to refer briefly to the writings of a most gifted observer of politics and politicians. The late F. S. Oliver, an Englishman, just before his death wrote a brilliant treatise in which he reflects: "How little the Art of Politics has changed in two thousand years!" [29] He goes on to say that "the predominant aim of politicians then, as now, was to rid themselves of their opponents, to gain power and keep it. Though our politicians use less lethal methods, their objects are still the same. Killing was then one of the recognized ways of getting rid of a dangerous rival, just as attacks on his public and private honour are today. But there was probably no more malice and hatred among the rivals then than there is now." [30] He points out that changes in fashion are very apt to be mistaken for a change in heart—that the death Lenin brought to the Imperial family and the middle classes in Russia is just as final as are the murders of treacherous confederates by Caesar Borgia. I might add that Hitler's deadly violence to his enemies in Germany and Austria, and Stalin's executions in Russia suggest that in the lands of the dictators killing is recognized as the certain method of removing those individuals of either high or low estates who are in the way. Probably the democratic state, with all its shortcomings, is the only place where there is personal freedom buttressed by the law of the land, and where no mere prince's will is the law. Mr. Oliver adds that as we look back toward the beginning of recorded history we find that it is not always the times nearest our own that are most like the present moment. "Those ancient Greeks are our coevals; they talk, and laugh, and scold as we do; vest themselves with the same problems; buoy themselves on the same hopes. . . . What, for example, do those Georgians [the men of Walpole's era in England] know about democracy: And what is there of this subject that Athenagoras, Cleon and Pericles do not know? And when we compare Athens of the fifth century before Christ with our own times, we cannot discover that politicians have increased since then in stature; or have changed their methods in anything essential; or that their characters have grown more virtuous; or that Democracy has undergone a transformation. In a broad view, the art of politics seems neither to have gained nor lost in all these years." [31]

There is one exception to the timelessness of Machiavelli on which I want to comment. He said in *The Prince* that a ruler should never interfere with the religion of his people; and yet Hitler has done that. Does this mean that

Machiavelli is wrong on this point, or that the situation has changed?

I think that the situation has changed, in this way. First, since the advent of the radio and the motion picture, the method of communication has improved enormously, perhaps a million-fold. Never before today has a dictator secured such complete control of men's minds as Hitler has. And secondly, Hitler has given the German people a new religion of Nazism in place of the religion of their fathers. The acceptance of this ersatz religion of Aryan supremacy culminating in Nazism was made possible by the control the dictator gained over the minds of the people because of the downward trend in religious values among the people that Hitler dominated, and by the weakness of the individual subject as compared to the organized armed might of the German State.

The German thinks with his blood—and that means no thinking at all, in our sense of the word. He reacts to commands. The American citizen is different. He is a citizen with a capital C, and his Bill of Rights in the fundamental law of the land, the Constitution, has erected a citadel around him wherein no government may enter. Within this fortress whose walls are the great civil liberties, the commonest citizen enjoys freedom of press, speech, religion, and assembly. But if one were to be permitted to retain only one of our four basic civil liberties (though the four are inseparable) the one that would have to be retained if democracy were to survive at all would be the right to openly discuss matters of government. The statesman in a democracy, and the ordinary politician too, is, first of all, a talker; he knows that the people like talk better than baseball—for he is an artist in human relationships; he, and not the professor or the psychologist, knows human nature. He understands the stresses and strains in a neighborhood, or a county, or in the big society, as reflected in a specific issue. He has a sixth sense that tells him where the bulk of the pressure lies. He sways with this pressure lest he be stopped in his tracks. Or he senses the inarticulate desire of the people to be led in some crisis on which they are free to express themselves—a crisis that requires leadership—and he acts accordingly.

Democracy is government by open discussion, and decision based on the opinion of a majority of the citizens. This holds for every unit in a democracy—from the small neighborhood communities and tiny town meetings, through the state and national governments. Talk is the stuff out of which the eventual decisions will come; and somehow the talk of a group of men and women who have the actual good of the free and humane at heart leads to something in the way of government that is the soundest thing men have yet known in their comparatively brief history as self-governing creatures.

Fascism and open discussion are incompatible, as the brilliant Ignazio Silone has unerringly observed:

Thomas the Cynic: . . . The only thing with which Fascism cannot be reconciled is clear ideas, and since these do not grow by themselves, like grass on the hillside, but are always *the result of discussion* between thinking persons, the only thing with which Fascism is incompatible is *discussion*. You must avoid discussion, Mr. W., like the devil holy water.

Mr. W.: And if I am challenged to a discussion and invited to give my opinion on an important question?

Thomas the Cynic: You will reply that no one can prevent you from fulfilling the mission entrusted to you by destiny.

Mr. W.: And if they ask me what my mission is?

Thomas the Cynic: You will reply that it is to save the country. "The country must and will be saved," you will say. "Nothing will prevent me from saving my country. No one can oppose destiny. That, brothers, is my mission."

Mr. W.: And if they ask me details about my mission?

Thomas the Cynic: You will reply, "My mission is to save the country. Destiny has entrusted me with that mission," and you can add that that is all you have to say to politicians, because your mission will be accomplished among the masses.[32]

*   *   *

On the brink of the Republican National Convention, the *Springfield Weekly Republican* for June 20, 1940, announced in an editorial that the people working for Taft's nomination had engaged 102 rooms in a Philadelphia hotel, the Gannett forces engaged nearly 50 rooms in the same hotel, and the group working for Dewey had taken 78 rooms in another hotel. These men and other men were preparing to run against President Roosevelt, "and of saying whatever they want to say about him. The aggregate floor space thus taken by those in opposition to him must run to an imposing total. *This is a vivid reminder that all the space available for anyone who openly opposed Hitler in Germany or Mussolini in Italy would be that of a grated cell—if not the still more restricted area of a grave.*"

FOOTNOTES

[1] II Samuel 15. (Italics mine.)
[2] The *Iliad of Homer*, I, lines 243 ff. (Lang, Leaf, and Myers translation).
[3] *Ibid.*, II, line 369 ff.
[4] *Ibid.*, II, lines 305 ff.
[5] "The Complete Writings of Thucydides"—The Peloponnesian War,

Book II, Chapter VI, The Funeral Oration of Pericles. Modern Library Edition. (Italics mine.)

[6] Henry A. Wallace, *America Must Choose* (Foreign Policy Association, New York, 1934), p. 13.

[7] *Ibid.*, p. 5.

[8] Walter Lippmann, *Public Opinion* (New York, 1931), p. 16.

[9] Quoted by John W. Studebaker, *Plain Talk* (Washington, 1936), p. 55.

[10] Norman Angell, *The Public Mind* (New York, 1927), p. 207.

[11] John W. Studebaker, *Plain Talk*, pp. 147-148. (Italics mine.)

[12] "Today, stimulated by these broadcasts, there are Town Hall courses in many large cities, and Town Meeting Discussion Clubs in homes, community centers, libraries, schools, churches, and wherever citizens gather. THE TOWN HALL, Inc., formerly THE LEAGUE FOR POLITICAL EDUCATION, has consequently set up an Advisory Service on a basis of self-support. Hundreds of discussion groups in thirty-one states are already using the service, with the number increasing daily. Members receive handbooks on discussion methods; weekly notices of programs; the magazine, *Town Meeting;* bibliographies and other information on program backgrounds; advice by correspondence on organization methods; and the book, *Town Meeting Comes to Town*, by Dr. and Mrs. Harry A. Overstreet."—From the description of the Town Meeting in the printed pamphlet of each broadcast.

[13] Robert M. La Follette, *A Personal Narrative of Political Experiences* (Madison, Wisconsin, 1913), pp. 336-337.

[14] *Ibid.*, p. 64.

[15] *Ibid.*, p. 65.

[16] *Ibid.*, p. 67.

[17] *New York Times*, June 25, 1938.

[18] *New York Times*, June 26, 1938.

The politician as a talker "domesticates the universal." He dramatizes the undramatic—the state, the government policy, the vast complex of laws and problems generally referred to as public affairs. But the politician, through the noble art of speech, does more than this: he engenders sympathy and understanding and relieves social tension. The politician in our democracy liquidates problems, conflicts, and divergent interests, not with bullets and violent death, but with skill of tongue and patronage and the ancient art of fixing. The politician as a maker of rules beyond rules is brilliantly described in *Politics and Public Service* (New York, 1939) by Leonard White and T. V. Smith.

[19] Nicolo Machiavelli, *The Prince* (New York, 1928), pp. 141-145.

[20] *Ibid.*, pp. 134-135.

[21] *Richard*, Act I, scene 4.

[22] *King Lear*, Act IV, scene 6.

[23] *Hamlet*, Act V, scene 1.

[24] *Second Part of King Henry the Sixth*, Act IV, scene 2.
[25] *Ibid.*, Act IV, scene 2.
[26] *Ibid.*
[27] *Ibid.*, Act IV, scene 6.
[28] *Ibid.*, Act IV, scene 2.
[29] F. S. Oliver, *The Endless Adventure* (New York, 1931), p. 86.
[30] *Ibid.*, p. 87.
[31] *Ibid.*, pp. 88-89.
[32] *School for Dictators*, pages 157-58.

CHAPTER III
"OF THE PEOPLE"

Taxpayers of Westchester County, N. Y., held a mass meeting last week in White Plains to protest the cost of their State Government. One speaker suggested that the Republican Legislature adopt a greatly reduced budget, let Democratic Governor Lehman veto it if he dare. State Senator Pliny W. Williamson (Republican) expostulated: "You wouldn't want the courts and State institutions and offices closed for lack of funds, would you?"

"*Yes!*" roared the taxpayers.

"Well," stammered the Senator, "if that's your attitude, I'm all for it." (April 17, 1939.)

My idea is that the politician is a human institution, that he is, was, and always will be the same—just as the basic pattern of human nature from the days of the Pharaohs to those of the Nicholas Fishbournes, the Charles L. McNarys, and the Maury Mavericks has not changed. The politician in our democracy is like the people, only more so.

A state senator in Wisconsin, a stalwart Republican, spoke to me on this point yesterday. "If you are going to stay in politics," he said, "you have got to be adroit enough to walk blindfolded across a floor covered with eggs, and never break a shell. You mustn't crack those shells because they are worthless things and would create a muss on the carpet." He paused, and then as an afterthought, "In addition, you must have the courage to go into that room and break every egg if need be, and, of course, when I say eggs I mean issues." Those who break the eggs have seemingly endless explaining to do. Save on rare occasions and in the case of unusually strong leaders, the eggs are not disturbed.

The incident about Senator Williamson dramatizes what is usually the sober procedure of the politician following the people, or those that are influential among them. The senator's uniqueness is in his recklessness in asking the question, rather than in his celerity in abandoning his reasonable opinion for one without reason. The standard politician never spits against the wind.[1]

*   *   *

And just who is the American politician? If I may, I shall repeat here my own definition. "The politician is usually a specialist in the art of governing, either in a neighborhood or in a nation. He is a person who takes a hand in nominating and electing himself or someone else to public office and who spends his time between elections in exercising and maintaining whatever political power he has cornered. He usually campaigns because he definitely wants to direct the course of local, state, or national government. In the majority of cases, however, the politician is as much interested in getting public recognition and in the excitement of political life as he is in the job itself; and his interest is neither casual nor spasmodic. Politics with him not only amounts to a profession, but actually *is* one." [2]

The above definition of a politician is, I believe, to a varying degree, descriptive of all politicians. Usually I count a man who has been elected to public office several times or more, a politician. Actually, I know that many politicians, and some very important ones, never hold public office themselves; they merely select the ones the people elect. And in some instances those whom they send are not politicians, but "order men," "fronts," "alter egos," "stooges," or merely messenger boys. For example, when Billy Campbell was register of wills in Philadelphia and leader of the 25th, he sent Jim C to Congress, and he told me that he could send anyone. "Why, professor, I could send you." (After I looked at Congressman C, I was confident that the leader could.) Congressman C would not talk to me at first. One day I found him in a spacious City Hall office with Bob Heinze, a leader very friendly to me. I explained my problem to Mr. Heinze. He said, "Jim, the professor says that you are afraid to talk to him. Now all of us talk to the professor." This roused the Congressman. He came up to me and shouted, "Professor, I ain't afraid to talk to you, or anybody like you. But let me tell you something. When I first went to Congress, one of the old hands there said, 'C, we don't know you, but we hear that you are all right. I have just one piece of advice to give. Remember this, *a man was never defeated by a speech he never made.*' And that is the reason, Professor, that I ain't talking to you." (Jim's most significant trait was loyalty. Billy Campbell and the Organization knew that he would do as he was told.) The Roosevelt landslide carried C out, and all of Billy Campbell's men have not, thus far, been able to put him back in. But there are always many C's in politics, though fewer now than in the years of prosperity. (But even in the days of Harding and Coolidge, when the party organizations were most powerful, the C's, or "order men," were rarely so limited in faculties and characteristics as Jim.)

When Nicholas Longworth was first elected to Congress, friends greeted him in Washington and congratulated him on his election. He, however, was vividly aware that a powerful organization in Ohio had put him there. He sadly shook his head and said to his friends, "Not election, appointment."

*   *   *

A leader is one who leads, and knows the ropes; a politician is one who knows the ropes. I observed Washington's birthday this year by talking for some hours to my friend Senator Coakley. Near the end of our discussion on politics and politicians, he unexpectedly exclaimed, "Why, J. T., you do not think I am a damned opportunist, do you? a wire-puller?" I reminded him of my definition of a politician—one who knows the ropes—and added, "Now, I suppose that some of these ropes are so fine that they seem almost like wires. If you are going to remain in public office, you must pay attention to matters of this sort." There was no answer to this plain statement, but the plainness of it was disturbing.

Knowing the ropes means knowing what it takes, whom to see, what to do, what to say and how to say it (and what not to say) in order to gain and hold office. The ropes on a sailing ship are taut or slack according to the wind and sea; and a politician campaigning must, like the sailor, fashion his ropes or techniques to suit the temper and size of his electorate. In a period of stress, when people are discontented, evidences of leadership are a source of strength. At other times and places the leadership may be provided by the Organization, and the winning candidate then stands mainly as a symbol of the party or of the status quo, and of the people who elect him. The politicians who get elected again and again are usually leaders, but of only a circumscribed sort. (Issues have destroyed personalities as well as parties.) It is surprising when one first studies the records of successful men in politics to learn how few, in normal times, can be identified with a controversial issue. If one considers our greatest office, the Presidency, and examines both the successful and unsuccessful contenders for it during the last hundred years, he is likely to conclude that a candidate's chances for winning here are in inverse proportion to his leadership in the field of controversial issues. The Jacksons, Lincolns, Clevelands, Roosevelts, and Wilsons are rarer than the forgotten men who held the office because they were available, that is, they had said nothing about national questions. On the other hand, Calhoun, Clay, Webster, Douglas, Greeley, Bryan, and La Follette provided leadership on national issues and were defeated. It seems wisest to say that a politician may be a leader or he may not be; the terms are not synonymous.

Probably the central point in this connection is that a politician is a vote-getter, and to the extent that getting votes requires leadership, the politician in a given case provides leadership (or he is pushed aside and one who can provide leadership is chosen).

In 1937 a group of political scientists were discussing the avenues of approach to politics. How might the university graduate get into politics? The varied answers revolved around the central idea of identifying one's self with a party organization. Then the eminent Charles Beard presented a different idea. He said that there was a milk strike in his community in Connecticut. He was asked to compose the difficulties in the situation. He immediately obtained all available books and documents on the milk question. He spent the night reading this material and in the morning he successfully brought a solution to the two conflicting parties. He added, "The newspapers hailed me as an expert on milk." Professor Beard then expressed the opinion that the way to get started in politics is to become identified with some community problem—take a position on some issue before the people: provide leadership.

On the other hand we are reminded of a statement made by Harding in his acceptance speech in 1920. He then said: "If men call for more specific details, I remind them that moral committals are broad and all-inclusive, and we are contemplating peoples in the concord of humanity's advancement." And he was elected by overwhelming millions!

*   *   *

National, state, and local politicians are all in the same business. One operates on a national level, one on a state level, and one on a county, city, ward or precinct level; but they have only one principle, or one object of allegiance—success at the polls. Whether or not the politician is of high or low estate, a gentleman with university degrees, a knave with university degrees, or a semi-illiterate boor; a Republican in Vermont, a Progressive in Wisconsin, or a Democrat in Georgia—he always has the same problem, the problem of gaining the attention of the people in his constituency so that they will vote for him on election day.

The manner in which he goes about garnering both the casual and the interested voter varies more as the electorate differs from some other electorate than as one politician is different from another. The pattern of politics has an inner core that is human nature and is more or less constant. Its fashions and outer manifestations change as the cultural environment, the economic status, the methods of communication, the density of population, the *Zeitgeist* and the climate change; but in a large sense the basic pattern of politics in a democracy remains the same from generation to generation.

To improvise on what I've already written, this body of knowledge that *is* politics is the folklore of all the city halls of the land; it is the living language of the county court houses, the vivid and real talk in the corridors of state legislatures, and the personal conversations on the fringe of Congress. It is the chosen topic at millions of firesides, dinner tables, working men's clubs, and saloons. It rivals the weather as a subject of conversation when two Americans meet. Much of it is as evanescent as smoke or as plum blossoms in the spring, but sometimes a word, an expression, or an idea is permanently fixed in the annals of the craft.

I

A basic fact about the politician is that he is like the people and knows what the people like. William Allen White, in 1936, said this was true of Landon. A majority of the voters disagreed with Mr. White's opinion, but I do think it is descriptive of politicians generally—the ones who are elected and re-elected to public office over a period of years. The politician is as he is because we are as we are. Theodore Roosevelt was probably the most American American of his time. Harding was described as "the common man to an uncommon degree." Now the common man may not himself know, but he may be able to discover who he is by the politician whom he elects. The people's choice is the mirror of ourselves against our own backgrounds. A candidate may be elected because he has the same faults and weaknesses that we have. *In our democracy we have representative government in a literal sense.* The citizen in the United States votes for someone like himself, or as he imagines himself to be, or as he would like to be. I do not mean solely as the voter might outwardly profess to want to be, but as in his secret heart he unerringly wishes to be. Of course, this is not true of everyone in the electorate or of every politician, but the politician who is elected term after term is likely to be as descriptive of his constituency as the sidewalks are of the streets. He is, however, likely to have special markings so that he may the more readily be recognized.

This identifying mark may be atmosphere, personality or a brown derby or both, as in the case of Al Smith. Or it may be a voice, or a manner of speaking (for example, a rural candidate may pull a wisp of blue grass and chew on it as he talks), or an expression of the folklore and folkways of the constituency. It is most likely to be one or more of these factors plus exceptional energy and stick-to-it-iveness in paying personal attention to the people.

If all the constituents in a district could be represented by a average color equally descriptive of all, their politician would be of that color too, only he would be of a deeper dye. Or to vary the figure, the politician would be of the same ingredients but a stronger flavor. He is "of the people" in the same way that the voters' religion, songs, entertainment, and vices are descriptive of them. He is an expression of their private loves and hates. Those of us who live a thousand miles from New Jersey may feel both indignation and wonder at the mere mention of Mayor Hague's name, or at news stories about congressmen or senators from other sections of the country. One day one finds oneself talking to the people of New Jersey about their mayor, and one understands. One may still be unutterably opposed to him, but now the matter makes sense; before it did not. One is reminded that the political climate, the economic situation, the cultural background, and the values in one community may not be those of another. The United States is a collection of those diverse and divergent communities. Each one chooses its politician after its own heart a good deal as a lady picks the man she marries. He may not be the perfect man, but he is the one she wants, or at any rate he is the one that she can get. Politics is like this. The art of politics and the art of love are not entirely disparate; logic is only one of the elements that determine the choice of voters and would-be brides.

The democratic theory of equality is traditional in the United States. This theory, buttressed by the stories of the Horatio Alger genre, encourages the voter to think that he is as good as anybody else. The idea of class is repugnant to the core of his being. When he votes, he votes for someone like himself, not someone better than himself. A one-legged man may run a better race in politics than would a Fenske or a Cunningham. The old story about the Republicans always winning the county clerk's office in a certain county until the Democrats produced a candidate with only one arm has some truth in it. A candidate with a missing tooth was successful, too. He thought that the people felt more at home with him than they would have had his smile been too different from their own. The one-time city clerk in Michigan City, Indiana, had infantile paralysis, and successfully campaigned in a wheel chair. A candidate will go far to remind the voter of his lowly and meagre start in life.

Sherman Minton once sold washing machines from door to door in Indiana. In demonstrating the machine he offered to do the washing for the prospective customer. Later, and after he had been elected to the United States Senate, he spoke the following words at a Democratic rally. "There may not be many who recognize me here tonight, but ladies, look close. Don't you remember me? Take a good look. Perhaps I am the one who did your washing some years ago. I was then selling washing machines in Indiana." A successful candidate for the office of Governor in 1938 said in a campaign speech, "Even when you call me governor at high noon, January 2, I will be the same plain, humble poverty-stricken boy you knew yesterday." The log cabin, dirt farmer, poor but honest, struggle for an education, are symbols that have helped many candidates into office. In addition, the candidate assiduously brushes elbows with the people, and if he is markedly superior in any way, his problem of self-effacement is all the greater. The most realistic candidate is going to try to make the voter feel superior— to inflate his ego.

Several years ago I talked to an old-timer in politics, one who was credited with having the best political brains in all Arcadia. We were talking about a politician named Smith, and I wanted the old-timer to talk about Jones. He said, "I like Jones." I answered that the people liked Smith better. "That's because," he quickly replied, "the people always like the horse's tail best. Now Jones is the smartest man in the state, and he acts like the smartest man. If I were the smartest man in Arcadia, I would act like the dumbest. I don't know about you, but when I was a boy we used to blow up frogs. Voters are like that. They like to be inflated." I recently discussed this question of voting for someone like one's self or someone better than one's self with Professor Laski. He said that he thought in England the voter cast his ballot for someone better than himself. "I have heard laboring people say, 'Why should I send him to Parliament? He does not know any more than I do.'" To what extent this remark is descriptive of political attitudes in England, I do not know. But if it is descriptive of people there, I should like to know if that is because they do not know social equality as we do here, or because they view these matters differently?

In December 1939 while visiting some friends in Michigan City, Indiana, I was asked if I wanted to meet a very interesting politician named Martin Krueger. Mr. Krueger was then eighty-one years old and he had three times been city clerk, six times mayor of Michigan City, and twice a member of the state assembly. I called at Mr. Krueger's home and he welcomed me cordially. He seemed remarkably fit for one of his years, and in a short time he was happily telling me the story of his life in politics, a life that covered a period of nearly sixty years. I mention it here because I am interested in pointing out the episodes of that life that illustrate the strength of the "of the people" factor in our politics. The fact that it was all casually told without any opportunity to plan makes the high lights stand out very clearly.

He began by describing the Tilden and Hendricks campaign year. He explained that Hendricks was from Indiana. "I considered Indiana my home, so I was very strong for Hendricks." He then described his first election to the office of city clerk. In this campaign, he was only twenty-three. The opposition charged that he was too young, that he never paid taxes, and that he was illiterate. In support of the last charge it was said that he had written a letter to a railroad for a farmer whose cow had been killed and that Mr. Krueger had spelled cow with a "K."

"I was told never to deny a charge, but to get around it. However, I discussed these three charges. In answer to the first, I said: 'It is said that I am too young. Now that charge might stick if it were brought against my father, but it can not be brought against me. I had nothing to do with it. Next, it is said that I never paid any taxes. That's true. I never had anything to pay taxes on, but I never had any difficulty in paying $2.00 or in getting plenty of men to work at $2.00 a day in place of paying taxes. The third charge that I spelled cow with a "K" is more important. But it is true. I spelled it that way because my mother in Mecklenburg, Germany, taught me to spell it that way. And that's the way you Germans spell cow now. K U H (Ka—oo—hah). You know that each of you spells cow the same way that I do.' " Mr. Krueger added that all of the people cheered and shouted, "Bully for you, Martin. You stick by the Germans and the Germans will stick by you." He explained that two-thirds of the Michigan City people at that time were German.

Mr. Krueger recalled a bet he had made on an election when Cleveland was a candidate for the Presidency. It was the campaign in which Cleveland was accused of having caused an unmarried girl to become a mother. The bet came up when one of Mr. Krueger's friends said that his German followers didn't know whom they voted for. Mr. Krueger bet that they did, and in order to settle the argument he picked out a voter and said to him, "Jim, how are you going to vote?"

Jim said, "Democratic."

Mr. Krueger replied that he knew that, but he wanted the names of the fellows that the man was going to support.

Jim said, "I am going to vote for the fellers on the Democratic ticket."

Mr. Krueger then said, "But who is the man?"

Jim thought a while and then smiled with assurance and said, "I am going to vote for the feller who had that girl in Buffalo."

I was unexpectedly reminded of the force of another aspect of the "of the people" element in our politics a few weeks ago while traveling on the Long Island Railroad. I found that the conductor intimately knew my friend Linnaeus, a man of about fifty, who lived near the end of the line. The conductor spoke well of him. I happened to remember that he had once been defeated for a political office in his small community. After hearing so much praise of Linnaeus, I reminded the conductor of the campaign and asked why my friend had been defeated. The conductor quickly gave me the answer. *"Linnaeus was not born in Cutchogue."* "But," I said, "he has lived there for twenty-seven years." Then with a superior smile the conductor replied, *"The man who beat him was born there."*

This inexorable residence requirement of all of our candidates, a requirement that insists not merely on present residence but often on long residence or even birth in a community or state of the candidate's constituents, is a basic factor in our politics. It is usually strongest in rural areas of the older states. It is everywhere important. One can imagine the voter's unconscious self saying, "The man who is going to represent us must be typical of our community. He must be representative of us in a literal sense—our occupations, language, climate, soil, and scenery. He is myself going into politics were I a candidate. He is me, but he cannot be me if he does not live here."

The average citizen would probably be unimpressed with the argument that our extreme residence requirement is one that steadily and persistently weighs against ability, character, and special talents, and supports those mediocre individuals whose strongest plea for office may be, "I was born here," or "I've lived here forty years." To see its leveling effect on the quality of successful candidates, one has merely to imagine how different Harvard or Columbia, or any other educational institution *would* be were it limited to Cambridge or New York in its choice of professors. The excellence of the educational institution may be gauged by the diversity of origins of its faculty. The same thing is true of private industry—Henry Ford or any other industrial concern looks to the far corners of the world, if need be, for the right man. A business that would employ only those born in that congressional district would be rather stodgy at the top.

Government and politics are not the same as either education or business, but the analogy still has real value. The problems confronting our politicians are so difficult that our best brains and strongest wills are needed. This may indicate that it might be wise to consider what a candidate is, rather than where he was born, in casting our ballots.

Another depressing fact, about this super-residence requirement, is the avenues to public service that it cuts off to capable politicians, who for one reason or another are unacceptable in their home constituencies. When Burke decided that the voters of Bristol were no longer sufficiently interested in his services, he withdrew as their candidate and stood for election at Malton. His parliamentary career, thus, instead of ending in 1780, ended in 1794. That this was fortunate, none will deny. (About one-third of the present members of Parliament in England were elected from districts other than the ones in which they have their residence. And according to the English Constitutional Year Book for 1938, eighty-seven members have been elected from two or more constituencies, four have been elected from four different districts. I mention this interesting fact about English politics because the greater mobility of members of Parliament must necessarily train their electorate to consider issues and a candidate's merits rather than merely his present place of residence or birth.) But how different the case of the American congressman who, because of an unpopular vote, is defeated in his own constituency. He cannot turn to another. He may be stopped on the very brink of his most useful service. One might also ask what effect does the knowledge of this residence requirement have on the minds and wills of American congressmen? Does this knowledge tend to make them weather-cocks or statesmen? The residence factor is not negligible.

*   *   *

Present conditions in the world demonstrate beyond doubt, however, that in spite of any or all excellencies that the English voting public may possess they, in the decade of the nineteen thirties, tragically failed to choose leaders wisely.

II

The importance of this aspect—the "of the people" characteristic—in our politics may be seen by observing the lives of either the great or the obscure, the great Lincoln or the unknown Nordhoff. The following descriptive passages from Carl Sandburg's *Abraham Lincoln—The Prairie Years* are in point.

"He looked like a farmer, it was often said; he seemed to have come from prairies and barns rather than city streets and barber shops; and in his own way he admitted and acknowledged it; he told voters from the stump that it was only a few years since he had worn buckskin breeches and they shrank in the rain and crept to his knees leaving the skin blue and bare. The very words that came off his lips in tangled important discussions among lawyers had a wilderness air and a log-cabin smack." [3]

The following picture of the candidate in action is interesting: "In campaigning among farmers, Lincoln pitched hay at the barns and cradled wheat in the fields *to show the gang he was one of 'em;* at various crossroads he threw the crowbar and let the local wrestlers try to get the crotch hoist on him." [4]

Finally, the very way Lincoln said "The People" identified him with the masses.

"He was their [the people's] thinker and spokesman. He knew what they wanted more deeply and thoroughly, more tragically and quizzically, than they knew themselves. He made them believe that he counted the political genius and social control of the masses of the people worth more in the long run than the assumption of those who secretly will not trust the people at all. He gained and held power, votes, friends, in many and far unknown corners and byways, because he threw some strange accent into the pronunciation of the words, 'The People.' He made them feel he and his like were 'stumbling-blocks to tyrants.' " [5]

Eugene Talmadge is a modern example of a politician identifying himself with the people. According to George Creel, Talmadge's favorite boasts are "that he has never been tired in his whole life, and that he knows every pig path in Georgia, and the majority of its citizens by their first names." Shortly after becoming governor he said:

"I am sort of city broke, but it is different with Mrs. Talmadge. Sunday morning she was up long before daylight and this morning it was the same way. At breakfast she announced that she was going back to see the cows and chickens." [6] This aspect of the Talmadge technique is most effective among the share croppers and tenant farmers of Georgia. The candidate's idea is to identify himself with the groups before him.

"Of the people" is a trait that is more descriptive of the tenor of the candidate's thinking than his clothes or habitat. Lincoln had it and so does Franklin D. Roosevelt have it. One was born in a log cabin, and the other is lord of a manor. But the significant point is that "Each of them," in the words of Max Lerner, "managed somehow to catch the accents and express the aspirations of the ordinary people of his day."

William Hale Thompson was three times mayor of Chicago. In the 1931 Chicago primary I heard him address several thousand negro voters in these words:

"Mr. Chairman, the Representatives of the Church, and my good, good friends! As Senator Roberts, your chairman, said, 'The Mayor cannot and does not have to brag about his black mammy.' But it might be well for you to know that when I was a cub in politics and just beginning, they nominated aldermen in those days in convention—the different ward conventions—and when I was nominated, who do you suppose nominated Bill Thompson? Did a white man arise to do the job? No, sir, a Negro, your now senator, Del Roberts [applause], is the man that arose in that ward aldermanic convention and put your mayor in politics." [7]

Another illustration of the "of the people" factor among the colored voters follows. In Baltimore, the colored people were going to have one of their own seated in the mayor's reception room, out in the public for all to see, and this person was to be his secretary. The mayor favored the appointment of a light-colored Negro who could pass as a white, but the dominant Negroes wanted a black one appointed to this position. There was some discussion and argument, but finally the people who wanted a black Negro appointed to this position were successful, and there was much elation in the camp of the blacks.

In a Milwaukee senatorial district in 1938 the Socialists captured the offices of senator, four out of four assemblymen, four out of four supervisors, and four out of five aldermen. The post that was lost is in a ward where unemployment is greatest. The non-Socialist alderman who won is a man of mediocre ability and uncertain character. He got elected by the following strategy. He was on relief during the campaign. His opponent, the Socialist, had a secure job. The non-Socialist twice made the rounds of each house in the ward, pushing doorbells. His plea was, "My opponent has a job, I am on relief. If you elect me alderman, I will be taken off the relief rolls. The taxpayers will be helped, and I will regain my self-respect." The people, probably because of the great unemployment in the ward, accepted his argument.

In the rural towns of Wisconsin candidates and voters meet face to face, and the "of the people" element in a successful candidate's appeal is invariably present. Gunnar Nordhoff in the town of Wiley with a population of several hundred families said, "I have lived in this town for forty-six years and one of the cheese factories is named after me. This seems to build up my personality, and my name is constantly heard and seen. I am regarded, therefore, as a pioneer, which of course is also a very great aid. I know them all; they all know me. You cannot really know how important this fact really is. I know what each person desires. I knew that their great sore spot was the roads, so I fixed them."

When asked how he campaigned, he gave the answer that I have received from many other town chairmen. "The reason the people vote for me is because of the work I do, and not the campaigning. I never campaigned, only slightly my first year. One does not need to campaign when he knows every family in the township, and they all know me. I have made my greatest vote-getting campaign when I built up the roads during my first year. These roads were too low before and were continually being flooded, and now they're 'damn' good ones—after I built them up."

Finally, he is a faithful church member, and about this Mr. Nordhoff said, "In my town, nationality and church affiliations are the greatest of assets. A person who didn't belong to the White River Lutheran Church or wasn't Norwegian wouldn't have a ghost of a chance in becoming town chairman. Nearly 100 per cent of the families are devoted church members and all but the cheesemaker, and one other exception, are Norwegians."

In campaigning where the candidate is from a different social stratum, as in the case of President Roosevelt, or of a profession that sets him off from the people, as in the case of Professor Josh Lee of Oklahoma, the candidate usually "out-Herods Herod" in his attempt to convince the lowly voter that he is one of them at heart. I was fortunate enough to see the campaign strategy in a senatorial primary and a run-off primary in Oklahoma in 1936. The speeches—and there were many of them—of Josh Lee, the winning candidate, were Oklahoma speeches aimed at the heart and taste and history of an Oklahoma audience. They would not have produced so many votes per capita in Maine, or in New York, or in any state very different from Oklahoma. That is, a speech to the electorate and an academic lecture to a class in a University must both be nicely suited to the political maturity on the one hand and the previous academic training on the other of the audience. To describe a speech is not enough; one must also describe the attention and response of the group to whom the speech is given. Here it is sufficient to say that Josh Lee's speeches elected him. A few excerpts from a political address given at Duncan—and all of Josh Lee's speeches were very much the same—will describe in part both the politician and the voter.

First, it should be noted that Mr. Lee was a professor of speech at the University of Oklahoma, and he is a very effective speaker. He has a voice that can bring tears or laughter. He has a pleasing face and a smile that looks fine and clean. (A young woman who had heard Gomer Smith, one of Josh's opponents, deliver a speech told him that his speech was wonderful, but that she was not going to vote for him. And when Mr. Smith asked why, she said, "Oh, I think that Josh Lee is just the sweetest man.") He was once ordained for the Baptist ministry. This religious background would mean more in votes in Oklahoma than in Pennsylvania, for example. Furthermore, as professor of speech, Josh Lee had for more than twenty years most assiduously accepted countless invitations to speak at little red schoolhouses, churches, and other meeting places. His speeches were not on politics, but were politics just the same, for Josh was preparing his way to Washington. As he said in his 1936 campaign—he "had covered Oklahoma as a mustard plaster covers an aching back." A young man, twenty-five years of age, told me that the most vivid picture of his boyhood was his recollection of Josh Lee speaking at his country schoolhouse on Dickens' classic, "A Christmas Carol." A school teacher said that after Mr. Lee had talked to her students in 1926 she had asked them to write letters of thanks and appreciation to Professor Lee. "Imagine my great surprise, when every single student that had written received a personally signed letter from Professor Lee in reply."

The opportune time for which Mr. Lee had planned came in 1934 when he was elected to Congress. Two years later he campaigned for the United States Senate. One night in June 1936 he addressed several hundred people from and around Duncan, Oklahoma, on the lawn of the court house. There were a band, a well-lighted platform, and seats for the people. After the music, Josh briskly walked to the platform, and after the full measure of the applause had passed, he waved down the remnant with up-lifted hands and said:

"I am going to stand down among you after the speech and shake hands just as long as anyone will shake hands with me." And then he partly turned to his pretty wife, who was on the ground, and who was simply and beautifully dressed in a white linen suit and wide-brimmed hat and said, "I want you to meet my wife." (Mrs. Lee was brought to the platform, smiled and just stood. She was gently led off the platform.)

Mr. Lee then spoke in support of the Roosevelt Administration and his plan to take profits out of war. The remarks in his speech that received the greatest applause, and there were many, are indicated by the following examples:

"The first time I ever saw Oklahoma, I was looking out of the back of a covered wagon, and the tongue of that wagon was pointing west." (The covered wagon is a symbol in Oklahoma.) [8] He identified himself with the farmers and said, "I got a modern farm. That is, a well-mortgaged place." (Many of those people could say the same thing.) He said that there should be a farm for every farmer, and added, "If you want the people to sing 'My country 'tis of thee, sweet land of liberty . . . I love thy rocks and rills,' then give them a chance to own some of those rocks and rills." He was grieved that the farmers were not getting more money for their produce. He said, "When I was young, I sold eggs at five cents a dozen. Why, just think of it! An egg is a day's work for a hen." He was troubled about the surplus cotton crop, and so were his audience. He inquired, "How many Chinese are there? Say 400,000,-000. Now they all wear shirts made out of cotton. If each of their shirt tails were lengthened only one half an inch, Oklahoma's surplus cotton crop would disappear overnight." There were few aliens before him, but many jobless. He said, "The government ought to deport all aliens who have illegally entered this country and give their jobs to Americans. Don't forget that there are 8,000,000 aliens here, and 6,000,000 of them have jobs." He referred to the last Republican administration and the many millions then without work. He declared, "When Hoover was President, the empty stomachs of the hungry people were flapping like a pair of rayon bloomers in an Oklahoma wind storm." Near the end of his speech he exclaimed, "I am my own campaign manager. My campaign headquarters are in the hearts and homes of you people of Oklahoma." As he drew near the finish of his talk the tremor of his voice increased. Some of the eyes in the audience were moist. "Friends, I want you to wear my colors for me now and on election day. If you do, I will wear your colors for you in Washington."

He got down from the platform as soon as he had finished speaking. There was much applause. A line formed and he began shaking hands and calling many by their first names.[9]

Governor Marland was also a contender for T. P. Gore's Senate seat, but he lacked color and oratorical powers. He realized the seriousness of these shortcomings, and did his best to make up for them. He persuaded the Honorable Jack Walton, a governor who had been impeached, and who has loads of color and what it takes to hold an Oklahoma audience, to introduce him—and the introductions were not short, though Governor Marland's speeches were. Much was done to convince the people that although Marland had once been a wealthy oil man, he was now a Roosevelt humanitarian, and above all, a genuine Oklahoman. There were about 8,000 people on the Capitol grounds one night in July 1936. There was a well-lighted platform with loudspeakers—the people were sitting on the ground or on benches. Jack Walton was briefly introduced by a Mr. Douglas who told this story.

It seems that Jack Walton's people were from Sugar Loaf Mountain, Arkansas, and that when Jack was a small boy they were so poor that they had no furniture at all. The only furniture that they had was the kind that Grandpa Walton could carve out of trees. All that they had was a house full of kids, a pack of hounds, and ten razor-back hogs. Life went on this way until one day Grandpa got some money saved and then he went to town and bought a wagon load of town furniture. Young Jack saw the team returning home, loaded high with things from the store. He climbed on the wagon and wanted to know the name of every article—bureau, chair, rug, and so on. Finally, Jack came to a mirror that was lying face up on the bottom of the wagon. He looked into that and saw his own features, and right away he exclaimed, "God, Grandpa, you bought a wolf too!" Right behind me I heard someone say, "I have heard that story a million times." And maybe he had, and maybe the rest of the people recognized it, too, but if they did, they welcomed it back as an old friend, for the applause was instantaneous and great.

Next to Oklahoma the people of the Sooner state like Arkansas best. Mr. Douglas then said that Jack Walton reminded him of the man in the story—"A preacher suddenly called on all of the congregation who wanted to go to heaven to stand up. Everyone stood up except one man, and when the preacher asked him why he did not stand up, he said, 'Well, I was thinking of going back to Arkansas, but if I am not able to do that, I will consider your proposition.'" Again there was much applause, and then Mr.

Douglas said, "I need not tell you people of Oklahoma who Jack Walton is, and what he has done for you—all of you know that: I am proud to introduce Jack Walton."

From the moment that Mr. Walton started speaking until he stopped, he carried the crowd. This was less on account of the things he said than the way he said them. The picture and atmosphere he created, the inflections of his voice, the use of his hands did the trick. The night was very hot, and he began by saying, "It's mighty fine of all of you people coming out here on a hot night like this. I know it is hot, for I was out walking on the prairie this afternoon. Out there I saw a jackrabbit being chased by a hound. It was so hot that they both were walking." The laughter that followed indicated that his audience had seen the grey streak known as a jackrabbit when it was being chased by hounds. Then he told a story about Douglas, and before the applause had ended he spoke at some length in support of Governor Marland and his administration. When the Governor addressed the crowd, the people were feeling very good. The Governor gave a more formal talk on what his and the Roosevelt administration had done and wanted to continue to do for the people. The voters on election day, however, decided that they would like to have Marland remain governor (his term had still two more years to go) and elected Josh Lee to the Senate.

Senator T. P. Gore, the blind senator, whose seat was being fought over, was badly defeated in this campaign. This veteran in politics lost because he no longer represented the basic attitude of his constituents. The Oklahoma people were in favor of the Roosevelt administration, and the Senator was thought to be hostile to it. Josh Lee, the winner, was said to have the help of many WPA workers, and this accounted for some of his strength when the ballots were counted, but the real explanation of his victory can be found in the indefatigable campaign that he waged and his success in making the controlling part of Oklahoma believe that he was Oklahoma.

These descriptions of part of the pattern of politics in Josh Lee's Oklahoma campaign reveal the ways in which the winning candidate is "of the people." They also indicate the value of a good speaking voice and inexhaustible energy; the candidate has the best chance who can speak to as many people in as many parts of the state as many times as possible. And the speeches must be the kind that first get the attention of the group and next the favorable support of the voter. Josh Lee was able to do all of these things.

III

The politician is apt to be of the same nationality and religion as is a controlling part of his constituency. No Roman Catholic, Jew, or Negro has ever been President of the United States, and none is likely to be. In 1928, Ellery Sedgwick, editor of *The Atlantic*, expressed the idea that in the coming presidential election some tens of thousands of voters would vote for Herbert Hoover, some hundreds of thousands of voters would vote for Al Smith, and some millions of voters would vote against Al Smith. I think that the prophecy was verified by the election returns. In addition to his religion there are two other factors that helped divide the electorate in the 1928 campaign. Al Smith is a son of immigrants from Europe, and a child of the city streets. Finally, he was identified with the wet side of the prohibition question.

In other than presidential elections the nationality and religion of the candidate may or may not be controlling. Here such factors as the genius of the candidate for getting votes, his record, or organized strength, his service to the people, his opposition, or a vivid issue may be the paramount thing in determining the way a vote is cast. But if one will examine the election returns, either in the rural towns and townships or in the city wards and precincts, he is likely to find that the Norwegians, German Protestants, German Catholics, Jews, Irish, Polish, Italians or others vote for one of their own. Assemblyman Andrew Biemiller came to Milwaukee in 1933. In 1932 the Socialists had been victorious in three out of four city-wide offices. The fourth was lost by a small margin. "I was curious as to why the fourth had lost. I asked an old German Socialist why. His answer was 'Andreas, that is very simple to explain. Our candidate's name was Bennohowicz. If we had had some one with a good old American name like *Schemmelpfenning*, we could have won.'" Mr. Biemiller is one of the strongest assemblymen in the state, yet he thinks that his German name is a distinct asset to him in his Milwaukee constituency.

If there are, for example, a dozen candidates of nearly equal strength in a primary, the winner is apt to be the one with a nationality or religion advantage." To cite one example that will stand for many: in a recent race for sheriff in Dane County, Wisconsin, there were 16 candidates for the Republican nomination for sheriff. In the Norwegian town of Christiania, approximately 252 votes were cast, 201 were marked for the Norwegian candidate Smedal and the other 51 votes were scattered among the remaining 15 candidates. In the town of Springfield, 312 votes, composed largely of

German Catholics and German Protestants, Staack, a German Catholic received 137 votes, and Burmeister, a German Protestant, was given 78, Smedal received 2, and the other 96 votes were scattered among the remaining 13 candidates. There are more Norwegians in Dane County than there are members of any other national group. Smedal won in the primary and again in the election. Smedal's method of campaigning was novel. He would be introduced at a meeting or a gathering in a farmer's yard, say a very few words, and play a tune on a Hardanger violin that he carried. The applause that followed usually led him to play again, and then he would modestly bow and retire without another word to the group. However, he would speak to friends and acquaintances both before and after his part of the meeting. Doc Deadman, an unsuccessful opponent of Smedal, described the campaign in rhyme. I quote the first four lines:

Hark, when Harold Smedal sings
Alcohol and ludefisk skoal be kings
Gammel-öost and flat bread and beer so mild
Goodness, won't Doc Deadman and Jim Brader be wild.

Nationality and religion are most likely to be decisive when no compelling issue is at stake. These factors, however, cast their shadow over all elections; yet, the more important the issue in any election, the less significant these factors are, for they are grounded in the subrational stuff of human beings—something that cuts deeper than rational experience. For example, in 1928 Al Smith did not have a chance of being elected because he is a Roman Catholic and there was no fear on the horizon. In 1932 the situation had changed, however, and voters were so disturbed by the status quo that they wanted a change. They wanted that change so badly that had Al Smith been nominated by the one major party in opposition he would, I believe, have been elected. When there is an issue, the voter is forced to think; when there is no issue the voter is more inclined to follow primitive symbols.

FOOTNOTES

[1] See my discussion of the idea that "every politician is subject to a great fear" in the introduction to *The American Politician* (North Carolina, 1938).

The Honorable Maury Maverick spoke with clarity and vigor during his days in Congress. But his days were numbered. He was defeated in his attempt for renomination in 1938. Right after his election to the office of Mayor of San Antonio, 1939, he exclaimed, "I'm going to be a stuffed shirt. I got beat for Congress for not being one."

Professor Robert C. Brooks has recently called to my attention a letter used by Pennsylvania's Senator, Jim Davis. As the *Philadelphia Record* pertinently remarks, this form letter is so nicely worded that it will cover "every situation from foreign entanglements to the cost of the Willow Dell Post Office." The Senator's letter reads:

"Dear Friend: I thank you for your letter expressing your views with regard to certain proposed legislation. In response, I should like to express an opinion in full on the matter you have brought to my attention. For the moment, however, I am prevented from doing this due to the volume of mail and numerous Senate duties that confront me daily.

"You realize, of course, that frequently certain provisions of a measure are so altered by amendments in either the committee or on the floor of the Senate as to change the real purport of the original bill. Hence the bill in its final form when I am asked to vote on it may be quite different from the bill to which you refer. However, your views in either event will be borne in mind and will receive my earnest and careful attention.

"I want to be of service to you and thank you for writing me.
"Most cordially yours,
"James J. Davis."

—*Philadelphia Record*, April 14, 1939

2 J. T. Salter, "The Politician and the Voter," in *The American Political Scene*, edited by E. B. Logan (New York, 1936), p. 89. See also *Boss Rule: Portraits in City Politics* (New York, 1935).

3 Carl Sandburg, *Abraham Lincoln—The Prairie Years*, Vol. I, p. 303 (New York, 1926). Harcourt, Brace and Company, publishers.

4 *Ibid.*, Vol. I, p. 161. (Italics mine.)

5 *Ibid.*, Vol. II, p. 199.

6 *Time*, January 30, 1933, p. 15.

7 Salter, J. T., "L'Élu du Peuple," *Révue des Sciences Politiques*, Vol. LIV, pp. 522-540.

8 Josh Lee was not unique in trying to convince his audience that he was Oklahoma—one of their very own, and a pretty nice one at that. One of his opponents, Gomer Smith, who courted the Townsend vote, proudly declared, "The blood of the Cherokee Indians flows in my veins." But there are five civilized tribes in Oklahoma, not counting the white people without Indian ancestry, and besides Gomer was too radical to win.

9 He gave a talk at a teachers' convention in Wisconsin in 1938 for a cash fee. This time as soon as he had finished his address, he disappeared. It takes both time and energy to talk and shake hands, and the Wisconsin teachers were not part of his electorate.

10 This feeling of national pride is indicated by the following incident told me by a state senator in Wisconsin. While campaigning in 1934 we were assured by an elderly Norwegian that the La Follettes were originally Norwegians. They had come from Norway and stopped over in France only long enough to assume the French form of their name.

CHAPTER IV
PERSONAL ATTENTION

"Well, in the first place, I'm an old-fashioned fellow who was brought up in a small town, who learned his politics in a small town, and who still believes that the only way to get ahead in public life is to understand people and to sympathize with their viewpoint. It doesn't hurt my feelings when some sophisticated gentleman of the writing craft describes me as the kind of fellow who likes to go back to the old home town and salute the neighbors by their first names while they greet me in return with a hearty 'Hello, Jim.' The radio is a wonderful thing—it has been a tremendous factor in promoting the success of the Roosevelt political fortunes—but, to my way of thinking, there is no substitute for the personal touch and there never will be, unless the Lord starts to make human beings different from the way he makes them now."—*Behind the Ballots* by Jim Farley, pp. 192-193.

Who is the American voter? What does he want? What determines his preference for Candidate Blodgett as against Murphy? Why does he vote for some politicians again and again, and pass by others who may be better educated, finer in appearance, and more honest?

A clue to one of the very significant traits in most citizens was disclosed in 1939 when the monarchs of England visited our shores. When the American sovereign voter was presented to the British King and Queen, Homo Americanus bent, curtsied or scraped with gusto, if not with grace. In his democratic heart he knew that the occasion demanded some special show of deference—some marked personal attention on his part. He would have had much the same feeling, but with less outer manifestation of it, had his own President, or Governor, or favorite political leader stood before him. All through history the approach to a King has been fashioned out of ceremonial and ritual.

But in the democratic United States it is the single voter that is sovereign, and he, like other sovereigns from time immemorial, expects his public servants to pay him the same sort of personal attention that George and Elizabeth so painstakingly bestowed on their American public. No ward or rural politician, stained by a life-long quest for votes, could have more effectively bestowed individual attention on constituents than did the British Monarchs in their few days here. They must have taken great pains, but they seemed merely graceful as they courted the people. Here Queen Elizabeth leans far over the side of her automobile in order to examine more closely the badge a girl scout is wearing; King George, sitting on the far side, cranes to see it, too. A seven-year-old presents them with a bouquet. The Queen stoops to take the gift, the King watches intently with a smile; both are absorbed in the moment. Not only the grave of the Unknown Soldier, but the Unknown Soldier himself, receives personal attention. The Queen remarks that she saw this man at Delhi. "I was a nurse." Thousands of hands were shaken; a hundred thousand smiles were given. Kings know what common people learn, that a smile is the same to all classes and to all parties; a smile is the best argument.

Who is the best vote-getter in the United States? Who is our smartest politician? What man in public office has most assiduously wooed the people—wooed them by speaking to them personally, by calling untold millions, "My friends"? Our President, Franklin D. Roosevelt, is the man. He has won the hearts of a controlling number of voters, by making them believe that he was thinking of them personally, when he gave his magical "fireside" talks. Each listener was likely to say, "He means me." The President carried his own message to the people; he paid personal attention to them, and they in turn voted for him on election day.

That is the standard formula for success at the polls, whether the office sought be in a neighborhood or in a nation, the office of town supervisor or President. In the pattern of politics—that is, in the elements or constants that occur and reoccur in every campaign, the factor of *personal attention* is enormously important. The American may be a lonely soul in the Great Society, but nevertheless he is one that likes to be recognized. He has a wish to feel important. He likes the idea of having in office a man that he knows—a friend of his. The good neighbor policy is a reflection of this attitude and it goes back to the time when strangers were spoken to on the street. The service club idea is a modern expression of the same thing. "I now introduce Mr. William Blake. Hello, Bill!" It is an expression of our equalitarianism, and of friendship. "The Governor and I, my friend"—when this official decides policies he has his friend in mind. The official that gets close enough to the people is responsive to their needs. And probably the instinct of the voter is sound. Every politician knows it's real. Why is the Honorable Philip La Follette glad to be called Phil? He knows that Phil can get votes that the Honorable Philip La Follette can not get.

This "personal motif" of our politics is best understood by the plain people themselves, and by those who have had dealings with candidates for public office. It seems to have escaped the attention of the majority of reformers and certain textbook writers. The discussion which follows merely represents my own opinion and belief in regard to one of the elements in our pattern of politics; however, the opinion and belief are based on both an intimate and rather long observation of politicians and voters, and all of my illustrations are examples taken from life. They might have been found in a politician's notebook (if he were ever to keep a notebook on those daily activities of his that go far in determining his strength at election time), and they are pages from the unchronicled lives of our people. Since my subject matter is human nature, the thoughtful reader will be able to fit what I write about into his own experience, having in mind, however, that I write of voters generally, the thoughtful and unthoughtful alike; all ballots have equal value when the votes are counted.

One time I lived at the home of a great singer. Her cousin, Miss Sherwood, a lady of ninety-one, lived there too. After several months I was unexpectedly stopped one evening in the dimly lighted corridor by Miss Sherwood. She asked, "Is it Mr. Salter?" And then, "Mr. Salter, I am glad that you live here." I said that I was too, and then asked why she was glad. "Because," she replied, "you make me feel important." And so it is with people generally. We like to feel important. And one of the most common and effective ways in which to make a person feel important is to single him out for personal attention. Moreover, if the personal attention is bestowed by a man in public office, its effectiveness is measurably enhanced. A recent remark of a fraternity student nicely illustrates this idea. "Ex-Governor Schmedeman paid me one of the greatest compliments that ever could be bestowed by just mentioning a single sentence and shaking my hand. I was at the Capitol with some fraternity brothers, idling about the corridors, when the 'Governor' passed by and called out—'Hey, Jim, I saw you jump "Grey Dawn" [a jumping mare] last week. Will you teach me to ride as well?'

"I was thunderstruck that the Governor should remember me—merely a contestant in a horse show, but in front of my brothers it was the most flattering thing that he could have said, and I grieve that I was not able to help him into office in 1934." But non-fraternity students feel just the same about this sort of thing. "The alderman of the ninth ward in Racine [Frank P. Marino] always calls me 'Carmine' whenever he sees me, and this makes me feel very important, especially when I am called that with my friends near by. I should add that I voted for him in Madison by absentee ballot last April."

A young minister is impressed at the sight of the mayor and his wife in his first congregation. "Chunky [the mayor] complimented me highly on the sermon. Mrs. Martin [the mayor's wife] came up after the sermon with tears streaming down her face." A treasurer in a small northern town told me that the farmers like to have their farms praised. Whenever he visited one, he made notes on its condition and then when he returned he could praise the improvements made. He added that the farmers were like brides who wished to have favorable remarks made about their cooking. A friend told me about a banquet, and added, "This was the first time in my life that I sat next to a congressman." On the occasion of a parade I heard an unknown say to an acquaintance, "I just shook hands with the mayor." I was reminded of the lady who had shaken the President's hand, and then declared that she would never wash that hand again. Years ago, our colored maid in Pennsylvania told me that she always voted for Mr. Blodgett because around election time he always said, "Good morning, Mary Jolly," and then she added, "That makes me feel good." Different people in Wisconsin, and at least one with a Ph.D. degree, have happily told me, "I got a Christmas greeting from Phil La Follette."

I know a farmer who invariably receives a Christmas card from Phil or Bob, and I know that he expects it. One year he failed to get the "Merry Christmas and Prosperous New Year" card and he was keenly disappointed. In spite of the perennial stream of greetings that went out from the Governor, I have never received one. When I first tried to obtain a copy for my file, I was told, "I would give it to you, but I had planned to keep it."

The story that Maurois tells about Disraeli is utterly foreign to our politics here:

Disraeli was walking up and down a station platform waiting for his train. The baggage master finally approached him, held out his hand, and proudly said, "Mr. Disraeli, I have voted for you for twenty years." Mr. Disraeli paused in his stride, looked at the hand, at the man, coldly shook his head, "I am sorry, I do not know you," and resumed his pacing.

In Henry Adams' biography of John Randolph he has a chapter entitled "Eccentricities." In that chapter I find this item (p. 257):

"How do you do, Mr. L? I am a candidate for Congress and should be pleased to have your vote."

"Unfortunately, I have no vote, Mr. Randolph."

"Good morning, Mr. L."

This attitude is certainly an eccentric one, even for the very eccentric Randolph of Roanoke.

The other examples I give are characteristic of the American pattern: A friend in Oklahoma told me about a congressman there who sent a letter of congratulation to her uncle when his sow produced a large litter of pigs. A young man in Mississippi married and at the conclusion of his honeymoon received a letter from his assemblyman saying, "I trust that you and Mrs. B. had a most successful honeymoon."

One of the time-honored methods by which politicians bestow personal attention is baby kissing. (I am not thinking of the Oshkosh mayor either, who when asked how he got elected, said, "Baby kissing." His boon companion observed, "But they can't vote." The mayor laconically replied, "The ones I kissed can.") I have never seen a politician kiss a baby, but I have often heard of it. And in *Pickwick Papers*, Dickens has given a vivid word picture of the Honourable Samuel Slumkey, candidate for Parliament, wooing the voters by this method *inter alia*. The conversation is between the candidate and his chief party worker, a Mr. Perker. The latter says:

" 'Nothing has been left undone, my dear sir—nothing whatever. There are twenty washed men at the street door for you to shake hands with; and six children in arms that you're to pat on the head, and inquire the age of; be particular about the children, my dear sir—it has always a great effect, that sort of thing.'

" 'I'll take care,' said the honourable Samuel Slumkey.

" 'And, perhaps, my dear sir—' said the cautious little man, 'perhaps if you *could*—I don't mean to say it's indispensable—but if you *could* manage to kiss one of 'em, it would produce a very great impression on the crowd.'

" 'Wouldn't it have as good an effect if the proposer or

seconder did that?' said the honourable Samuel Slumkey.

" 'Why, I am afraid it wouldn't,' replied the agent; 'if it were done by yourself, my dear sir, I think it would make you very popular.'

" 'Very well,' said the honourable Samuel Slumkey, with a resigned air, 'then it must be done. That's all.'

" 'Arrange the procession,' cried the twenty committee-men.

"Amidst the cheers of the assembled throng, the band, and the constables, and the committee-men, and the voters, and the horsemen, and the carriages, took their places—each of the two-horse vehicles being closely packed with as many gentlemen as could manage to stand upright in it; and that assigned to Mr. Perker, containing Mr. Pickwick, Mr. Tupman, Mr. Snodgrass, and about half a dozen of the committee besides.

"There was a moment of awful suspense as the procession waited for the honourable Samuel Slumkey to step into his carriage. Suddenly the crowd set up a great cheering.

" 'He has come out,' said little Mr. Perker, greatly excited; the more so as their position did not enable them to see what was going forward.

"Another cheer, much louder.

" 'He has shaken hands with the men,' cried the little agent.

"Another cheer, far more vehement.

" 'He has patted the babies on the head,' said Mr. Perker, trembling with anxiety.

"A roar of applause rent the air.

" 'He has kissed one of 'em!' exclaimed the delighted little man.

"A second roar.

" 'He has kissed another,' gasped the excited manager.

"A third roar.

" 'He's kissing 'em all!' screamed the enthusiastic little gentleman. And hailed by the deafening shouts of the multitude, the procession moved on."

Some modern politicians have gone far beyond the Slumkeys and legendary ones who kissed infants. When the secretary of the Honorable Frank B. Keefe learns that a baby is born in the 6th Congressional district of Wisconsin, he sends a most useful pamphlet of 107 printed pages, clearly written and fully illustrated, entitled *Infant Care*. It is publication No. 8 of the Children's Bureau in the Department of Labor. Accompanying the book is a list of other government publications on the care of the mother and child, that may be had for the asking, and the following letter typed on Congressional stationery:

Dear Friends:

I have just learned of the arrival of a new visitor in your home and take this opportunity of extending to you my congratulations and best wishes. May the little one bring to you much joy and happiness.

I am sending you under separate cover a booklet on "Infant Care," which I trust you will find of help in solving some of the problems with which you will now be confronted. Having helped to raise three of my own, I know what a responsibility you have on your hands, even though you will be more than repaid for all your efforts.

With every good wish, I am

Sincerely yours,

Frank B. Keefe, M.C.

This sort of attention is worthy of a statesman. Fortunately, it is regarded as such by an overwhelming number of parents.

Birthdays, Christmas, deaths, and weddings are standard occasions when politicians pay personal attention to the voter. But there are innumerable other times and situations, not marked on any calendar, when the resourceful candidate is able to make some voter feel important, to identify himself with some voter, or group, or to do a personal favor for a voter. An assemblyman who has been elected many times said, "It's not the big issues that cause the trouble in politics, it's the details—the little details." More than one congressman has painfully learned that his recommendation for postmaster at Broken Bow has more bearing on his next campaign than does his vote on national policies. The trivial things are interesting: often the questions that interest the voter are not important. Senator Greenquist said, "If there is a vote four miles away, go after it. Do not neglect a single vote. My barber was too busy to leave his shop on election day. I swept the place while he voted." And then he added, "I never get a haircut in Madison. I always go back to my district." A councilman in ——— told a professor that he spoke to everyone. An observer interrupted and said, "You even spoke to me." He answered, "Of course I did. If I didn't speak to every son-of-a-bitch I meet, I would lose my job. Your sins may be many in politics, but if you speak to every one they will be forgiven."

Sol Levitan has six times been elected treasurer of Wisconsin. The following comment was written by a university student. It seems to indicate that a smile is a smile regardless of education or religion.

"Then came good old Sol Levitan. For years I had heard my Dad talk about him. Once many years ago when my Dad and I were in the Capitol, we paid Sol a visit. He let me sit at his desk and even let me hold a bundle of money just so I could see how it felt to hold such a sum of money. At the time I was too young to have any interest or knowledge about politics. Now I am for Sol and, although my Dad is a good Republican, nevertheless, from that day on he always voted for Sol Levitan whether he ran on the Republican ticket or the Progressive ticket."

In normal times some people will not vote unless they are personally invited to by the politician of their neighborhood: other people require transportation to the polls before they cast their ballots. I know politicians in Philadelphia who chartered busses in the 1920's in order to bring voters in from the shore to register. Hitler's Germany paid traveling expenses from Chicago and other points in the United States to Germany in 1935 in order that German people here might vote on the Saar plebiscite of that year.

However, since the Great Depression has been upon us, the voter's interest in his government (his ballot) has quickened. One politician in a metropolitan area complained to me in a letter that he knew that the 1936 election was bad for him and his friends, because his voters came to the polls in droves. He went on to say that when one must drag voters out, the party in power feels safe, but when great numbers of people come to the polls under their own power, it means defeat.

Another way to point out the great significance of the personal attention aspect of our politics is to ask this question: What is the most commonly used method of getting

votes in any or all of the 120,000 or more precincts in the
United States? Isn't it buttonholing voters? Isn't it meeting the voter face to face and saying (but not so brazenly),
"I am a candidate; will you vote for me?" I think that it is.
The candidates, or their representatives, who see their constituents at different times throughout the year, are
stronger than those who call only at election time. And if
in addition to *seeing* the voter, the candidate or his *alter
ego*, the party worker, does something for him, isn't the
candidate—other things being at all equal—in the strongest
possible position? Finally, isn't this sort of approach to the
sovereign (but often dependent) citizen a controlling part
of the explanation of the victory of Tammany, Hague,
Pendergast, Crump, and other powerful organizations at
the polls? And when these organizations are defeated, isn't
that the result of their failure to satisfy needs? It probably
is, plus the additional fact of a dramatic, dynamic Roosevelt
or La Guardia on the other side who has not only the
"goods" but the great histrionic ability needed to show the
people that they are in a position to give the voter more
for his money (ballot) than will any rival firm.

James Farley signs many of his letters merely "Jim"—
and in green ink. He is perhaps unique in using green ink,
but he follows the standard pattern by signing the informal
"Jim." To many people the most interesting writing that
they ever read is their own name in print; and the Honorable W. H. Goldthorpe so strongly believes this that he
has prepared a special green postcard, one side of which
is for the address and the other side is divided by a vertical
line. The left side of the card is blank and on the right side
in black and red type is printed:

Clipping Bureau

W. H. GOLDTHORPE

Your Assemblyman

Dear Constituent:

The appended clipping from one of our exchanges may be of interest to you, as it is to me. With that idea in mind, I am sending it along to you with my compliments.

With Best Wishes,
"GOLDY"

Your
Assemblyman

This assemblyman explained that he takes all of the newspapers from his assembly district, looks through them, and when he finds a news item that Mrs. Norski entertained the Ladies Aid at her home on Tuesday evening, he clips and pastes it on the card, and mails the card to Mrs. Norski. The assemblyman smiled and said, "The people like it."

Mr. Goldthorpe has another form card that he uses in sounding out the sentiment of the people on proposed legislation. The form is a double postcard with a perforated line separating the two. He briefly describes, for example, a measure requiring cold storage eggs to be so labeled. He asks if the person is for or against the measure. His picture is on the left-hand side of the card that bears the person's address. Above the picture are the words, "Assembly Chamber, Madison, Wis.," and below, "Just plain 'Goldy' (Your Assemblyman)." On the card that is to be returned to him, his name and address are given in an informal fashion that might delight Jim Farley—

—just plain, "GOLDY"

(My Assemblyman)

MADISON,

(Assembly Chamber)   WIS.

"Goldy" has an eight-piece band composed of members
of his own family. He explained to me that during campaign time he will go to a meeting in his district and ask
the voters if they want to hear hot air or hot music. "You
see that is all most political speeches are anyway." Usually
the people say "Hot music." "We play 'She'll Be Comin'
'Round the Mountain When She Comes,' the 'Beer Barrel
Polka,' and other popular pieces."

His most effective piece of campaign literature is an
orange-colored blotter. Although it does not indicate the
party to which Mr. Goldthorpe belongs, nor does it take a
position on any controversial question, it does unquali-
fiedly take a stand on the golden rule. Every effort is used
to get the personal and favorable attention of the voter. I
quote the document in its entirety.

Re-Elect Your Old Friend

W. H. GOLDTHORPE
(Just Plain "Goldy")

ASSEMBLYMAN

ONE GOOD TERM DESERVES ANOTHER

————————

Keep Saying: "GOLDY"—My Assemblyman
He's Tooted For Us—Now Let's Toot For Him

Over on the left third is an eight-page leaflet, about two by two inches in size, entitled "Thumbnail Sketch of Goldy —Your Assemblyman." The first two pages are captioned "General Information." I quote:

Born September 2, 1880. Graduate of Platteville State Teachers College. Studied Law and Advertising. Newspaper Publisher for 35 years. Married Ina Grindell, a Platteville Girl. Father of 10 children. Assemblyman for a Term and a Half. His Platteville Band Serenaded Pres. McKinley; Recommended by the late Teddy Roosevelt. Taught School and was President of the School Board.

The third page is headed "Platform." It contains three words:

THE GOLDEN RULE.

The fourth page, "Philosophy":

"Teach a Boy to Blow a Horn and He Won't Blow a Safe."

The fifth page is blank. It is entitled "Jail Record." The last page is headed "Finger Prints." Below are three finger prints.

Goldy's band helped him get elected to the assembly. In Texas, W. Lee O'Daniel was chosen governor in 1938, and although his campaign technique cannot be described by any one word, yet neither can it be described without mentioning the fact that he campaigned with a Hill-Billy Band. The significant fact here, as in many other similar cases, is not merely that the successful candidate may be one who devotes his best energies to capturing the attention of the voter, entertaining the voter, making him feel good; the question is—does the candidate discuss the issues, too? The candidate may make a statement on a controversial political issue, or he may not. Candidate O'Daniel made political speeches, and he invited the people to ask questions, but when a searching question was asked, Mr. O'Daniel would often say, "We will now hear from our Hill-Billy Band."

A politician is a physician of the body politic. If an ordinary physician to a voter's body—a plain M.D.—were asked an opinion about the cause and cure of a pain in the voter's anatomy, the doctor would not be expected to burst into song, or to render a violin solo, or even to bring his band to the home of the patient or to the hospital, and play a piece. Neither would the doctor answer that he stood squarely behind the Ten Commandments. In getting a medical practitioner's opinion, the patient may merely get pink pills, but he accepts them because he thinks that they will help him. They are relevant. But the political practitioner, at certain times, and in certain districts, is not bound to give a relevant answer; he is not necessarily required to give a logical opinion; he is apt to do what must be done to woo the voter—to get the voter's support. What it takes to do this depends more on the voter than on the politician. The voter sets the standard—the politician comes up to it. Voters crave personal attention. That is the reason *personal* attention is an important element in our pattern of politics.

Every politician has something of Goldy and his band in him, but that is not the question. The real point is: what else does he have? Here is a United States senator who returned to his home town and found some of the town's people laughing at a young man who was working night and day on a homemade aeroplane. The first time it was tested it did not leave the ground. But the senator paid the boy a personal call, congratulated him on his ambition, and got him some pertinent literature from the aeronautical research division of the federal government. This helped the boy to get his plane to fly; it helped the senator in the minds and hearts of many people, even those who had laughed; and it especially helped him with the boy and his relatives. Finally, in addition to much personal service work of this sort, this man is an outstanding senator in his own right.

The examples of personal attention and service are as numerous as the problems in all the lives of all the people in a community. In the small town of X there was a foul odor in a certain neighborhood. One of the families investigated and found the source of the horrendous smell to be the one out-door privy in that section. This family complained to the alderman. He immediately left his business and visited the scene of the great stench. He was able to get the owner to dispose of the offensive building within two days.

Or the politician may administer the law so as to please some constituent. Two years ago a person in a small city did some plumbing work in his own home. An ordinance was passed which prohibited any one other than a registered plumber from doing this work. The city clerk was campaigning for re-election. The situation was explained to him. The clerk did not give this plumbing ordinance official notice until the interested family had completed its work. I should add that in November the six votes in that family went for the incumbent city clerk.

*   *   *

Politics is one of the most strenuous trades men follow. This is partly because there are so many people to see personally. A man drove up to a farmhouse and asked to see Mr. Hendricks, the farmer. His wife thinking that the caller was a salesman said that Mr. Hendricks was out in the fields and could not be bothered. The man was not to be stopped, for he started to walk across plowed fields and cobblestones to see Mr. Hendricks. When Mr. Hendricks returned home, he told his wife that the caller was the district attorney of Waukesha, who was thinking of running for Congress. He added that it was merely a friendly call, for all they had talked about was the crops.

Personal attention, as I have said, is sometimes merely a smile, a handclasp, a word of greeting; usually, however, it is part and parcel of personal service, a favor done for a voter. I can illustrate this best by describing three experiences in the recent political campaigning of Laurie Carlson, a Progressive of Bayfield County, Wisconsin. Laurie is about thirty years old. He is serving his second term in the assembly, although he looks younger than many college seniors. His handsome boyish appearance nearly cost him some votes. An old Swedish woman with many relatives told him that he was too young for the assembly job, but the old matriarch became a strong supporter when he answered her in Swedish.

In 1936 Laurie found that several important farmers were opposed to him, and he needed their support in order to win. One of these farmers was Ernest Tetzmer whom Laurie visited one day in the country. He found Mr. Tetzmer out in the hayfield cocking hay, and Mr. Tetzmer said that he was already committed to another candidate and could not support Mr. Carlson. Laurie talked to him just the same, and while he was talking he noticed that the ground was very dry at the foot of a hill. He asked if there were not some seepage or springs in that hill. The farmer thought there was. Laurie then suggested that they take a look at the springs as a possible source for irrigation. They did and Laurie made some pertinent suggestions about taking out the muck, damming the springs and piping the water down to the farm for irrigation purposes. The next day Laurie got some helpful advice from the University and relayed it on to the farmer. A dam was constructed, and land that had been useless is now profitable. Naturally the farmer feels that if you can make a blade of grass grow where none grew before you deserve his vote.

The next case concerns Sam Kransovitz, who is an influential man among the Slovak people of his community. Laurie met Sam at a Slovak church picnic and found that Sam was not for him. The two drank a couple of beers, and then Sam invited Laurie over to his home for supper that evening. Laurie quickly accepted the invitation, and at the end of the supper Sam and his wife went out to the barn to milk cows and told Laurie they had no time to talk politics. It was in August and very hot. Laurie was dressed in a sport coat, white flannel trousers, and white shoes. However, he followed the farmer and his wife to the barn, took his place among the cows, and milked five. One of the cows had a very wet tail, and because the flies disturbed the cow, the wet tail switched across Laurie's face many times during the milking. It cost Laurie $1.50 to get his clothes cleaned after the session in the barn; but from that time on Sam has been a supporter of his. Again no politics were talked, but political support was won just the same.

Laurie is very much interested in music and so is Jonas Pearson, a Swedish hermit, who was opposed to Laurie's candidacy. One afternoon Laurie drove out to his farm. Mr. Pearson asked Laurie to come in, and at once the candidate noticed a heap of musical scores and etudes and a grand piano and a pipe organ. They talked music, ranging from contemporary composers to Beethoven and Mozart. After the talk had progressed for a while, Mr. Pearson played a few selections from notes and then Laurie played from memory four or five classical numbers which he had learned. From that day on Mr. Pearson has been a strong supporter of Mr. Carlson, although, again, politics were not mentioned.

Although this personal attention motif is most important in small constituencies where it is physically possible for the candidate to greet all of the voters, it is not to be ignored anywhere. Carl Zeidler, an inexperienced young man with a baritone voice, an eager handclasp and a memory for first names, this April defeated Dan Hoan, one of the greatest mayors ever produced by an American city. During the twenty-four years that Dan Hoan was Mayor of Milwaukee that city was better governed for a longer period of time than any large city in America. The city won more blue ribbons, gold medals, and first prizes for its fine administration than any other city has ever won. Yet this municipal statesman was defeated by a handsome boyish fellow who spoke three hundred times a year, and on some occasions four times in one night. He would make a speech or sing a song more easily, and more frequently, than some people greet an acquaintance. Zeidler joined many organizations and, in addition to singing *On the Road to Mandalay*, he cultivated the nationality groups by singing in Polish, German, Italian. The day after the election his father said, "I expected him to win. I'll tell you why. There are 40 nationality groups in Milwaukee and Carl knows every one of their leaders and many of the rank and file— They elected him." A veteran office-holder said, "The young people did it. They wanted a change." There are other factors, but the one that most fully explains Zeidler's victory is his smile and the enormous amount of personal attention that he bestowed on the voters.

But according to Dan Hoan, his defeat was caused by a world-wide condition, one expression of which is the 16,000 boys and young men in Milwaukee who have never had a job. And then he added, "I suppose two-thirds of the people in Milwaukee have never known anything but good government."

Two successful politicians worked most effectively together in bestowing the coveted personal attention on their constituents when the Honorable Robert M. La Follette gave a speech in the fall of 1938 in the assembly district of Paul Alfonsi. The district is in the northern part of Wisconsin and is composed of Italians, Poles, Finns, and some Norwegians. Several hundred people attended the La Follette-Alfonsi rally, and after the speaking was over they waited to meet the Senator. About three hundred voters formed a line, with the assemblyman and the Senator at its head. One by one, as they filed by, Alfonsi called each voter by name and introduced him to La Follette. No matter how good the speech, there were many constituents in the line that thought the handshake at the end the best part of it.

I know an assemblyman who needed the support of a certain clergyman in his district, and who, when this minister was going to be in Madison, arranged to have him open the assembly and the senate with prayer. As a result of this the pastor got his name in the newspaper and was paid $6.00 by the state.

This personal attention and personal service factor in our politics is universal. It is present in the little neighborhood and in the wide nation alike. How big a part it played in the life of Mark Hanna when he was leader of the Republican party in the Senate is vividly portrayed by Thomas Beer.

"He had woven himself into the life of the Congress. And how? Well, he was a business man in politics. Let some Congressman run to him with the case of a shipmaster bullied down at Buenos Aires by the venal authorities of the port, and Mr. Hanna's telephone clicked. The Senator was speaking to the State Department, to Mr. Hay himself. Let some Democrat approach him in the Marble Room wailing that Hay and the President were dragging the United States into world politics too far by demanding open door for the trade of all nations in China, and people drew close to hear Hanna retort, 'For American trade.' Nothing was too small to interest the Senator from Cleveland. He adjusted anything that was business. An engine driver had been crippled while helping to unload supplies at Tampa for the Army? All right. He would look after that, for Mr. Oscar Underwood, and he lectured the tall gentleman from Alabama on the dignity of engine drivers. 'I've talked to hundreds of 'em. Never met one fool, either. . . .' A cargo of mahogany, the sorrows of an insurance company shut out of Germany, the complaint of a lady whose son had been reprimanded at Annapolis for trying to invent a new torpedo, the inefficiency of a laundry machine in a government hospital—bring him anything that touched his instinct of a trader or that had to do with a machine, and Mr. Hanna's voice would be loud for the persons in trouble. A thousand such obligations bound Senators and Congressmen to Uncle Mark. He rose, in this simplicity, by his usefulness, and superstition clustered on him. He was luck, he was force—and there was something else. Dazedly and unwillingly, people came to see that the old jinni loved his country, and he queerly loved his city and his state. It was unaccountable, almost indecent, when he had been dramatized as a mere plunderer. But there it was. 'I won't have an American abused,' he growled, in the State Department, 'and I don't give a damn if he has a jail record and ain't got a cent. You get those Swiss to let him loose.' " [1]

II

I have spoken elsewhere of the personal attention and personal service aspect of politics in a metropolitan area. (See my sketches of ward politicians in *Boss Rule: Portraits in City Politics*.) The statement of one of the leaders is descriptive of many. "I work for you 364 days a year, all I ask you to do is to work one day for me." This is reducing the political process to very simple terms. It is my opinion, however, that this attention and service principle is basic and universal—it varies as the needs and intelligence of voters vary—it is not restricted to any one class, section, political party, or to great cities. (It should be understood, though, that some politicians use the personal attention technique in their attempt to carry on a comprehensive social and political program, and others use it without any great objective in view.) The point here is, that all men who get elected and re-elected to public office in our democracy, whether their objectives are public or private, devote a substantial amount of their time and energy to paying personal attention to their constituents. Edmund Burke tried to tell the voters of Bristol in 1780 that he canvassed them through their affairs and not their persons. But this was not good enough, and they rejected Burke. In order to present a more comprehensive view of this matter—of personal attention and personal service—I shall now describe in some detail the activities of certain members of the assembly in a particular rural state. Although the state that I have in mind happens to be more politically mature, and invariably better governed than the majority of states, I always refer to it as *Everystate*.

*   *   *

The legislature is organized early in January. At this time, members of the majority (and often minority members too) are able to reward one or more of their most valued helpers or friends by assisting them to secure positions as legislative employees. Even though Everystate has one of the oldest, and sometimes one of the best, state merit systems to be found in the United States, yet even here a friend is a friend, and if the friend is an assemblyman (or something bigger) he can help a deserving jobseeker connect with the public payroll.

Groups of school children and their teachers from different sections of the state often visit the capitol. Their assemblyman is apt to be on hand to greet them and to provide guides for a tour of the building. When a group appears in the gallery of the senate or assembly, its representative in the legislature may celebrate that fact by announcing its presence to the body, which may applaud. Then, if the member is particularly interested, he may have its visit recorded in the daily journal, and send a copy to each student and teacher with his compliments.

The Journal of the Assembly for April 27, 1938, contains the two following items among others:

The pupils of the following schools and their teachers were guests of the assembly:

> Woodlawn School, Wannette
> DeForest Graded School, Clinton
> Monroe School, Shaunee
> Valders Public School, Bolder
> Graphic Arts Club, Chickasha
> Packwaukee Study Club, Cushing County
> Open View School, El Reno
> Sunny Hill School, Noble
> Spring Valley School, Yale
> Clyde School, Manchester

RECEPTION OF RESOLUTIONS FOR REVISION

Mr. S. asked unanimous consent that Res. No. 42, A., be privileged and read at this time. Granted.

Res. No. 42, A.,
Granting the use of the assembly chamber to the Everystate High School Forensic Association for the annual high school speech contest.

WHEREAS, The Everystate High School Forensic Association has requested the use of the assembly chamber and parlor for the evening of May 9, 1939, for the annual high school speech contest in which the district winners of the state will participate; now, therefore, be it

Resolved by the assembly That the use of the assembly chamber and parlor is hereby granted to the Everystate High School Forensic Association for Monday evening, May 8, 1939, and Tuesday afternoon and evening, May 9, 1939, for the purpose of holding the annual high school speech contest for the district winners of the state.

By Mr. S., adopted by unanimous rising vote.

Before the students leave the building their legislator may present each child with a candy or ice-cream bar. When one assemblyman found that his special group was planning on a picnic at a near-by park, he ordered several cases of soda pop delivered there for them.

At innumerable times during the session the legislator is able to help his constituents by seeing state departments, commissions, administrative officials in behalf of some voters. Usually the assemblyman serves by cutting red tape, and thereby hastening the action desired by the voter back home. The legislator is able to do this because he helps enact the budget appropriation for the department—and besides he may know the administrative official personally.

A few characteristic examples will further explain the point. A truck operator came to the Capital to see his assemblyman about a problem over license fees. The ——— Division was insisting upon administering a part of a law that the trucker had failed to obey. The assemblyman went to the division, explained the situation, and in less than an hour the trucker was happily on his way home.

The Public Service Commission holds many hearings each year concerning utility rates, bus rates, trucking operations, and other matters. Testimony is taken down in shorthand, and some months may pass before the commission hands down an order. The intelligent attention of a legislator here, in behalf of interested constituents, often speeds up action on a pending case. I mean that an order may be issued sooner than would otherwise have been the case had no interested legislator spoken. It is merely an illustration of that very old idea of having a friend at court.

The Conservation Commission carries on an extensive fish-planting program. Many legislators are able to help their local Izaak Waltons secure supplies of fingerlings for the streams in their districts. A word from an assemblyman may mean better service, increased quantities, or better varieties, of fish.

All through the session the members receive hundreds, even thousands of requests from the people back home who are not able or willing to come to the State Capitol. They merely write letters. Legislative pages spend hours on many days in digging up information, collecting data, delivering messages for legislators. A corps of stenographers is usually busy typing letters for them, and sometimes a particularly energetic member may have four or five stenographers working for him at one time. Prompt attention to letter inquiries naturally enhances the good will for an assemblyman among his people.

Many members of the legislature introduce bills and resolutions at the request of interested constituents. The state prepares the draft and prints the bills. The author of a bill frequently wishes to secure extra copies of his foster child for distribution in his district. Using the privileged method, he secures adoption of a resolution providing for so many copies of reprints. He then sends copies back home.

JOINT RESOLUTION
Relating to additional copies of Bill No. ......

Resolved by the assembly, the senate concurring, That the chief clerk of the assembly be and he is hereby directed to procure the printing of five hundred additional copies of Bill No. ......, relating to regulation of milk dealers.

Joint resolutions are introduced in the legislature for a variety of reasons. A member may want to celebrate the memory of some prominent citizen who has died. I am quoting merely the first four and last four lines in a statement forty-four lines in length. I have omitted proper names.

JOINT RESOLUTION
Relating to the life and public service of ....

Mr. ...., village president for nine years, former assemblyman, and outstanding community leader of ......, Everystate, died January 8, 1939, of an infection resulting from an unfortunate fall. . . .

Resolved by the assembly, the senate concurring, That this resolution be spread upon the journal of the assembly and that properly attested copies of this resolution be sent to the members of the family of the deceased.

Or a legislator may want to congratulate some individual

or group in his district for some recent and noteworthy accomplishment. Resolutions of this sort are widely publicized at home; the action of the legislature is appreciated by many. I quote the first and last parts of the joint resolution.

JOINT RESOLUTION No. ......
April 11, 1939—Introduced by Senator .... Adopted.

JOINT RESOLUTION

Commending the debating teams and coaches of the High Schools of ......, ..., and ...... for outstanding performances in the State Debate Contest of the Everystate High School Forensic Association.

Whereas, The debating teams of ...... High School and ...... High School were declared tied for first place in the annual debating contest of the Everystate High School Forensic Association in the State Capitol, March 1, 1939, a circumstance never before recorded in these statewide tests of forensic skill; and . . .

Resolved, That copies of this resolution duly attested be transmitted to the principals of the ...... High School, and the ...... High School, and to the coach and the individual members of each such debating team.

Another member is interested in the growing strength of the old-age pensioners. He introduced a resolution memorializing congress to do something for the aged.

JOINT RESOLUTION No. ......
January 24, 1939—Introduced by Senator .... Referred to Committee on Legislative Procedure.

JOINT RESOLUTION

Memorializing the Congress of the United States to reduce the age limit to sixty years for old-age assistance.

Whereas, There are many needy and disabled persons in Everystate between the ages of sixty and sixty-five years whose wants are equally as great as of able-bodied persons over the age of sixty-five years and who must be provided for and supported by the state or its various municipalities; and . . .

Resolved, by the senate, the assembly concurring, That this legislature memorializes the Congress of the United States to amend Title I, Social Security Act of the United States, so as to reduce the age limit from sixty-five years to sixty years and to enable states to receive aid from the federal government on the same basis as such states now receive aid for assistance to persons over sixty-five years of age under such Social Security Act; Be it further

Resolved, That properly attested copies of this resolution be sent to the President of the United States, to both houses of Congress and to each Everystate member thereof.

Another valuable aid to certain members is the privilege of sponsoring certain important administration bills. Members who seek higher offices, or who face stiff battles in the next election campaign back home, may be given the opportunity to introduce a key bill. Or a bill may have several authors so that several members may bask in the majority-giving sunlight of publicity. Some people think that Assemblyman B will be a candidate for attorney general next election. This session he is the author of the widely discussed B—— Labor Bill.

A standard method in building good will among the folks in one's district is to send them state publications in which they are interested. Legislators have ready access to large numbers of a variety of reports, pamphlets, bulletins, documents, laws, maps, and papers printed by different departments. Many legislators secure several hundred copies of the new highway maps from the highway commission for distribution each year.

The Department of Agriculture and Markets puts out an attractive and informative bulletin No. 2000A. Various members have sent hundreds of copies of this publication to teachers, school children, libraries, clubs, and other interested individuals in their districts. These copies usually bear the stamp of the sender, notifying the recipient that he receives the document with the compliments of his legislator.

One of the most widely known documents furnished by the state is the annual Blue Book. A law was recently enacted increasing the number of Blue Books available to each member to —— copies. These are given to interested constituents, and if additional copies are required, they can usually be obtained.

The pamphlets containing the latest fishing and hunting laws and regulations are often in demand. Many legislators secure copies of these publications and send them to conservation clubs and other interested people in their districts. To lawyers and business firms legislators often send publications from the tax commission, the industrial commission, and other bureaus. At least one assemblyman sends out the session's bills as they are enacted into law to every lawyer in his district—about twenty-five of them. (The official price for this service is $5.00.) Still other members send out complete sets of all legislative documents to particularly interested constituents. (The official subscription price of this service is $25.00 paid to the secretary of state.) Teachers and school officials, town, city, and other local officials, tavern operators, and barbers, may each receive public documents of particular interest to them. One particular assemblyman secured from the department of public instruction the name and address of every school teacher in his district. He sends these school teachers pertinent documents issued by the state.

The following letter from State Senator X to his constituent, Doctor P., suggests that some legislators will steal for their voter in a pinch. I am reminded of a county commissioner in Philadelphia about whom a commentator once said, "Jimmie, X would steal the Liberty Bell if Bill Vare asked him to." Here is the letter:

Dear Doctor:

Under separate cover I am forwarding a 1937 Blue Book, which is sent at your request.

You will note that it is a very special book, with leather trimmings on the back. I had it made up especially for you.

I am also still trying to get you a set of 1937 statutes and will forward them as soon as possible. *I virtually have to steal them.*

Yours very truly,

Professor Merriam said that one time a bill was introduced in Congress for a Hennepin County canal. The canal never got anywhere, but the man who introduced the bill got re-elected to Congress. And so it is in Everystate. If a member introduces an appropriation bill here for some individual or group, he is likely to make new friends because of the publicity that he receives back home. This is true even though the bill fails.[2] In certain cases a pressure group may succeed in getting an appropriation bill passed by the legislature and signed by the governor. A pertinent example is a bill passed this session which appropriates $500 to a post of the Morning Glory Division, War Veterans of —— Everystate, for aid in paying convention expenses of 1939 and 1940.[3] If the veterans' organization opposes an assemblyman or senator in a campaign, his problem of getting re-elected is made more difficult in some cases, and made impossible in others.

Other appropriation bills passed this session provided for the payment of $10,000 to the Disabled American Veterans to promote a national convention and $50,000 to the American Legion for their national convention plans. About these appropriations a leading local newspaper stated editorially, "Republicans, Democrats, and Progressives vote for appropriations of this kind because politicians are always afraid of pressure groups. They vote for these appropriations when they know they are nothing more than a racket, because they fear honest opposition may cost them votes."

Certain members may become widely known because of some controversial or attention-compelling measure that they sponsor. An excellent example of this is the very great publicity that one assemblyman received this spring because of his Married Women's Bill.[4] Another method by which a legislator may gain favorable publicity back home is to introduce a bill adding portions of county roads to the state highway system. Even though the bill does not pass, and it probably will not because of added expenses to the state, the voter is apt to feel a more friendly attitude toward his representative.[5]

In the 1937 session, Bill 425A provided for an additional

thirty miles of paved roads to be added to the state trunk highway system in each county. The bill also provided that the respective county boards were to decide the location of the roads to be paved. Immediately the legislature was flooded with at least thirty-five amendments designating the roads that should be added to the state system. Although the bill was defeated because of these amendments, each of the thirty-odd assemblymen could go home and say, "I tried to pave this road for you." Assemblyman X devoted his best efforts to log-rolling in that session, trying to get U.S. Highway X which runs through X County transferred from one county to another. Assemblyman X worked strenuously for this measure for local reasons. He would approach a fellow legislator and promise to vote for anything provided the other legislator would vote for his road bill. His bill was passed. Assemblyman X voted for the governor's suggestion to end the legislative session. He was against a special session. But a few weeks later he returned to the governor's office and demanded a special session. When I asked the reason I was told, "Do you remember X's road bill; well, the bill provides for the paving of the wrong road, and he wants a special session to get the road bill passed all over again."

Legislators receive free passes to all university athletic contests, to certain theatres in different parts of the state, to the junior prom, military ball, and the state fair. Some of these passes are given to constituents.

A number of legislators prepare a weekly news letter for newspapers in their district. This gives the assemblyman or senator an opportunity to help educate the voter about what is going on at the Capitol and elsewhere, and to remind the voter of his representative under the big dome.

Lengthy debates on the floor of either house may be staged for the benefit of publicity back home. The facilities of two state-owned radio stations are available to all members at certain times. Legislators give fifteen-minute talks during week days when the legislature is in session. Some of these talks are mainly educational in value; they all give the speaker another opportunity to bring his name before his people.

In a survey of this sort, in which I briefly describe a few of the representative activities of the state legislator in personally serving the voter, I am painfully aware that I have barely scratched the surface. I know this because I have used only a fraction of my own materials and observations on the matter. Furthermore, my own data are everywhere most incomplete—like a bucket out of the sea. I have described these compelling personal attention activities as I have observed them and as they have been told to me by legislators and their close acquaintances. I think that many of these activities and services are exceedingly useful to our citizenry. I do not say that each act enumerated here is done with an eye single to the vote. It may be, or it may not. Why does an individual smile? Who knows? But we do know that certain individuals smile more than others, and the politicians who best succeed are—nine times out of ten—those who smile and do a favor for a friend—and their friends are very many. Some of these individuals would be friendly and helpful, whether or not they were in politics. Actually the ones who have this flair for making friends, and helping people, often gravitate to politics.

Most old-time politicians who have been at it for forty years or more, and who tell about their start, and their life in politics, are likely to say that they "brushed elbows with the people." When the first La Follette, for example, was a candidate for governor, he had to depend on his friends to help him get delegates. Many of these friends did not have any money either. They might live on a loaf of bread and sleep a night or two in a haystack, while away from home talking to delegates, but they did bring back the delegates. When Old Bob saw these friends in the capitol, or anywhere else, he sometimes threw his arms around them and kissed them, so great was his joy and his gratitude. He never changed. And if some one remarks that his son Phil is not like that, the answer is simple. How can he be when he has had none of these tell-tale experiences that stamped the imprint of the people upon the very core of his father's heart and experience?

Now although I believe that the smile must be genuine to be really effective, I also know, with Shakespeare, that one may smile, and smile, and still be a villain. One reason for this, I believe, is that politicians, like many other people, are likely to be sentimental. They may like the people, and like to see them around; they might give them a quarter, or help them get a job, and yet they might give a franchise to a private utility without securing adequate compensation to the city, or they might share in the profits of a contract that defrauds the public. I think Jimmie Walker, for example, likes people, but I do not think that he would make a good custodian of the public's monies. The politician is human. Whether or not he is honest cannot be determined by the quality of his smile, but the smile is apt to have something important to do with his success in politics. And the individuals who succeed here are rarely those who approve of Sir Walter Raleigh's poem:

> I wish I loved the Human Race;
> I wish I loved its silly face;
> I wish I liked the way it walks;
> I wish I liked the way it talks;
> And when I'm introduced to one
> I wish I thought *What Jolly Fun!*

The smile must be a real smile, not a mere grimace. It is an outward sign of some inward state: it is not a mere surface manifestation put on for convenience; for if it is, the people will recognize it as such and count it dross. I know a very handsome man who holds an appointive position. One day in his office, I observed him meet a citizen who was a comparative stranger. The face of the appointive individual lit up like a 200-watt bulb—for an instant—and then he turned it off and on again. The caller left. The owner of the electric smile turned to me and said, "That gets them." But it really doesn't. He holds an insignificant place in the affections of the people. It is simpler to fool the voters about the budget than about the integrity of a smile.

I know one assemblyman who made up his mind in the middle of the legislative session that he would never seek re-election again. For the remainder of the 1937 session he neglected his mail from his district, and didn't bother to send out the materials that he formerly sent out. I also know of another case in which X was elected to the assembly in 1932, the year of the Democratic landslide. He has been elected every time since then, and he works increasingly hard to keep in close contact with the people of his district. He, like many other members, makes frequent trips to the capitol when the legislature is not in session in order to serve his people.

Again I notice that the assemblyman who is defeated after only one term is likely to be one who neglected to pay this personal attention to the voter. And of course there are a few legislators who are unusually capable and effective as leaders, and these rare few may devote their time to the state's business and survive. But these gifted members are the exceptions, like Carter Glass, and their lives are not descriptive of the overwhelming majority of the men elected and re-elected to public office, whether it be in a neighborhood or a nation—and whether it be Mr. Blodgett or Vice-president Garner.[6]

Moreover, and even in the case of the strongest assemblymen, the real leaders, these personal attention activities are not neglected. Take the case of Brownlee. When his party is in power Brownlee is the speaker. He is eloquent on the stump, compelling in debate, has the energy of a La Guardia, and is a clear thinker. He stands for specific economic ideals that he discusses before the people of his district and elsewhere. Yet no assemblyman works harder in doing personal services for his voters than he. Every week he is before some commission obtaining a contract carrier's license, or fish for lakes, etc. He is also extremely alert to the administration of WPA in his district. Furthermore, bills introduced that may be of interest to special groups in his area are dispatched to the interested groups as soon as the bills are printed. And finally, there is no assemblyman who spends more time at the state capitol between sessions than does Brownlee.

The situation is somewhat different in the case of an assemblyman who is securely, or closely, identified with some powerful group in his district. It does not matter what interest is represented so long as it can command a controlling number of votes. It may be an iron or copper mine, a railroad, a dairy or farmer association, a labor or party organization. In other districts there is no one organized group so powerful as to be able to decide the outcome of elections. Some years ago I was talking to a Pennsylvania senator who said that he had to return to Reading to consult his constituents on a pending piece of legislation. Nathan Stanbury, a senator from Philadelphia, where the party organization is—or was then—all-powerful in politics, spoke, "I can very easily see my constituents, for I have only one—Ed Vare."

An assemblyman from the one big city in Everystate, who represents labor and enjoys strong organized support at the polls, is freer from these personal attention activities, but he cannot neglect labor leaders. He explained his situation to me in these words:

"In my own case, I am constantly sending copies of bills to labor leaders, particularly those leaders in whose unions large numbers of members reside in my district. I also make a special point to answer every communication I get from a labor union, partly because I have been advised by the outstanding labor leaders of this state that it is important to constantly keep my name before every union. However, I am perfectly willing to admit that I do some of the personal contact work with constituents that you mention. Every assemblyman does. For example, this year one of my precinct leaders sent me the names of one hundred and fifty fishing enthusiasts in my district. I sent each one a copy of the latest fishing laws along with a personal letter wishing them a successful season, etc. To my pleasant surprise, I received about fifty letters of acknowledgment. I expected a few, but to get about one-third! I think this is a good illustration of the point made by you regarding the inflation of the ego of the voter. I found that lots of fellows will do more for copies of fishing laws than a present of $100. It makes them feel important. They can go around showing the laws which say, 'With the compliments of——.' "

Finally, there are two additional comments that should be made. The politician is an exceedingly useful—not to say indispensable—institution in our democracy. Some of the needs that he satisfies are recognized in formal political theory; others are part of the unwritten constitution of politics,—vital, sometimes controlling, but not mentioned in the constitution and statutes. In this latter connection, it is as though an individual called at a law office for legal aid. The attorney gave, or did not give, the desired help, but he did give his client a cigar. Or we may say that a doctor was visiting a patient suffering from malaria. The physician did or did not help the person who was ill, but he did repair a broken rocking chair at the patient's home. These analogies have merit, but they are not exact, because the client seeking legal aid and the patient expecting medical attention knew pretty well the sort of thing that they wanted. Politics is more ambiguous. The issues and the methods to be employed are rarely clear. Furthermore, the physician has a certificate of his training and general competence that is issued by the state; the lawyer has a comparable certificate; but there is no equivalent diploma of so exact a nature for the politician.

My second idea revolves around the voter. In our democracy the voter more often than not is likely to have a sense of ego instead of a sense of state. This means that he is apt to see the common good—if he thinks of it at all when he votes—in terms of what is good for him personally, privately, and individually. That this attitude may lead to a dangerous situation is evident. It is as though the purchasing agent for a city were to buy from those firms that gave prizes to the agent. All will agree that this procedure would sacrifice the public interest. Nor would any court of law permit the defendant or the plaintiff to give a present to a juror. Yet in politics, and even though a smile may disable a voter, candidates who are successful invariably campaign with smiles, handclasps, and other remembered acts of personal attention.

If I may depart from my role as observer and "lecture" for a moment, I would say something like this:

It is the nature and wishes of the voter that determine how the politician performs on our political stage. The truth is that vast numbers of the voters are ordinary petty politicians themselves. The meaning of the ballot should and must be redefined before things can improve much. The voter must be educated to think in terms of community and merit instead of self and favors. [These words are so easily written and yet so difficult to put into practice. A wife can rarely reform a husband—my wife wants me to abandon my pipe!—How then can a civic worker reform a voter? It is the hardest of all hard tasks to educate a person to be as concerned with a more distant future good for the group than he naturally is with his own private advantage on the spot.] The voter must vote for a candidate because of his interest in the common good, and the belief that the vote he casts will best serve the state. He must realize that the candidate of his choice does not owe him *anything for his vote that he does not owe all people in his constituency. If he is intelligent, he understands that his vote is given to the state, not to an individual. It is true that he places his X after a candidate's name, but he is thinking of the state. He is actually trying to pick a state's man, or a city's man, not a voter's man or a private interest's man. Therefore the voter deserves neither a $5.00 bill nor a job nor a Christmas greeting for his vote, nor can he rightfully give it away. All he can intelligently do is to cast it according to the dictates of his own conscience— which should be re-inforced by a knowledge of the facts involved.*

Since this is a country in which individuals matter, and can express themselves freely, the chief responsibility of us all is to make ourselves and our children fit for such freedom as we have, by bearing in mind that here the individual is important, and that his ballot is not merely important, but indispensable to him, as the old flintlock and powderhorn were indispensable to his forefathers who fought the Indians. But the ballot is permanently valuable only when the citizen achieves a stature and a vision that enable him to look beyond his immediate private interest and see the common good. In a profoundly fundamental sense a citizen with intelligence (whether he is selfish or unselfish) will more and more think of the state when he votes, for in that way he will most powerfully strengthen his own position. A man without an effective state in these days of 1940 and organized and collective action is about as helpless as a cub without a mother. Man is a political animal now infinitely more truly than he was when Aristotle described him as such. The state is the chief instrument of the lowly voter in securing and maintaining the good life for himself and his children. If that life is dear to him, let him hold his ballot dear. It is his weakness or his strength, and no one can vitiate that strength or take it away so long as he votes for candidates who support the common good.

FOOTNOTES

[1] *Hanna*, pp. 234-35, by Thomas Beer. Printed by permission of the publishers, Alfred A. Knopf, Inc.

[2] I quote the following bill in its entirety, save for proper names.

No. ......

March 2, 1939—Introduced by Mr. .... Referred to Committee on Judiciary.

A BILL

To appropriate a sum of money therein named to Edward S. and Alvin S. of the town of ...., ... County, to reimburse them for hogs killed by bears.

The people of Everystate, represented in senate and assembly, do enact as follows:

SECTION 1. There is appropriated from the general fund to Edward S. and Alvin S. of the town of ...., ... County, Everystate, the sum of two hundred dollars to compensate them for damages sustained by reason of the killing of twenty small pigs and four large pigs by bears. Acceptance of this appropriation shall operate as a full and complete release to the state on the part of Edward S. and Alvin S. on account of such damages and expenses.

SECTION 2. This Act shall take effect upon passage and publication.

[3] I quote the following Act in its entirety, save for names.

To appropriate a sum of money therein named to the Everystate Chapter of Morning Glory Veterans for annual conventions.

The people of Everystate, represented in senate and assembly, do enact as follows:

SECTION 1. There is appropriated from the general fund to the Everystate Chapter of Morning Glory Veterans of ...., Everystate, comprising veterans primarily from ......, ..., ..., and ......, the sum of five hundred dollars, for the purpose of defraying a portion of the convention expenses for the years of 1939 and 1940. The sum of two hundred and fifty dollars shall be paid on August first of each of such years to the then acting secretary and treasurer of such Everystate Chapter of Morning Glory Veterans.

SECTION 2. This act shall take effect upon passage and publication.

4   No. ......

January 31, 1939—Introduced by Mr. ...., Referred to Committee on State Affairs.

A BILL

To create section .... of the statutes, relating to married persons in service.

The people of Everystate, represented in senate and assembly, do enact as follows:

SECTION 1. A new section is added to the statutes to read: .... STATE EMPLOYMENT OF MARRIED PERSONS. No married person shall be employed in the service of the state or of any political sub-division thereof who has a husband or wife regularly employed at a salary of more than fifteen hundred dollars a year plus four hundred dollars for each dependent child, or whose income, together with that of said husband or wife is two thousand dollars, plus four hundred dollars for each dependent child. This section shall not apply to charitable and penal institutions or married persons employed therein. This act is emergency legislation.

SECTION 2. This act shall take effect July 1, 1939, and shall continue in effect to July 1, 1943.

5

No. ......

April 28, 1939—Introduced by Mr. ...., Referred to Committee on Highways.

A BILL

Directing the state highway commission to add to the state trunk highway system a certain highway approximately nineteen miles in length completing a state trunk highway from the city of .... to ....

The people of Everystate, represented in senate and assembly, do enact as follows:

SECTION 1. The State highway commission is authorized and directed to add to the state trunk highway system a highway extend-

ing from .... to ...., following the course of what is
known and designated as county trunk highway U northeast and east
to the intersection with county trunk highway G, then north along
county trunk highway G to its intersection with county trunk
highway Q, thence east along county trunk highway Q in .... and
...... counties to its intersection with county trunk highway H to its
intersection with county trunk highway A, then east along county
trunk highway A into the city of ...., thence over what is now
designated as state trunk highway one hundred and forty-nine in
.... county to state trunk highway one hundred and forty-one,
thence east over county trunk highway F in .... county to ....
....

SECTION 2. This act shall take effect upon passage and publication.

[6] I find the following item in a recent newspaper. "The House folding
room got its biggest job of the congressional session the other day—
mailing out 1,000,000 copies of a speech boosting Jack Garner for
president.
"Sent under the frank of Garner's crony, Representative Milton H.
West of Texas, the campaign splurge will cost taxpayers approximately
$5,000.
"Author of the highly esteemed opus is Roy Miller, wealthy Texas
oil lobbyist and Garner's campaign impresario. Miller delivered the address before a gathering of prominent Detroit businessmen. Later Representative West inserted it into the congressional record (at a public cost
of $55 a page) so it could be printed at cost in the government print-
ing office and then mailed free.—*The Capital Times*, June 1, 1939.

CHAPTER V

LEADERSHIP

It is a mistake to believe that the enthusiasm of the masses depends on the value of the men who lead them. The truth is just the opposite—the social value of the men who lead depends on the capacity for enthusiasm which the mass possesses. In certain periods the soul of the people seems to shrink. It becomes sordid, envious, petulant, and its power of creating social myths is atrophied. In the time of Socrates, for instance, there were certainly men as strong as Hercules could possibly have been; but the Greek soul had cooled and was no longer capable of creating glowing myths that wove the twelve great labors into a golden belt and set it in the sky.—*Invertebrate Spain* by José Ortega y Gasset, pp. 61-62.

What is leadership? Each one knows what it is, but no one has ever adequately described it. The great imaginative novelists have written about love, but only men without great imagination have tried to tell us what leadership is. To describe it requires the sort of genius that one would need to explain why Tom caught fish and Dick didn't. These two brothers had a vacation on a lake in the woods. They had a boat and every day they rowed out in the lake and fished. The first day Tom caught eleven bass and Dick caught none. The second, third, fourth, and fifth days were the same. Tom caught a fine string of fish, but Dick, using the same bait, caught none. On the sixth day Dick asked Tom to stay home. He thought that if he were to go alone, his luck would change. On that day Dick fished alone, right where Tom had made his catches day after day, but still Dick was without success. Finally, he reeled in his line and started rowing for the shore. Just then a big bass jumped out of the water and shouted, "Where's your brother?"

This question "Where's your brother?" is the sort that is bound to come up whenever one thinks of leaders and followers. The leader may or may not be educated; he may or may not be intelligent; he may or may not be good; but he does have something, some quality that draws his followers to him as a magnet draws iron filings.

This something is a life-force plus. It is an extra charge of vitality and conviction. In some cases it seems to his followers a kind of human thunderclap from the gods—by which I mean, something with a touch of the miraculous and unprecedented, that suggests elements beyond the realms of reason and the workaday world. In any case there is apt to be in a leader this center or spark of vitality that is both more intense and abundant than that which most men possess. It is usually something that is deeper down than the rational processes; it is a kind of super "it," a colossal "oomph."

Right at the start, when we think of leadership we might ask who is the greatest leader that ever lived. We in the Western world who are of the Christian tradition are likely to feel that the greatest man the earth has ever known was Jesus. But his kind of leadership, although in at least three ways it revolved around elements that are basic in the technique and equipment of leaders today, was in essence and scope something set apart, not only in degree but also in kind.

Judged by our typical leaders he was a failure. He never controlled a majority; he sacrificed himself rather than ask the lowliest follower to lose his life. He planned for eternity, and he had no mortal success. He was taken by the authorities and crucified, and his tiny group of followers fled when the crisis came. His influence was infinitesimal until after his death. And he had in his lifetime nothing that even approximated an organized following.

But he had three characteristics that lesser leaders of this world invariably have too. One was personality—or the magic charm that made the sons of Zebedee drop their nets and follow him for life. It was something that was more important to his followers than anything else in the world. He said, "I am the way, the truth, and the life." A few people saw that at once; increasing millions have later come to feel it, or at least to say that Jesus is the supreme truth. This faculty to evoke something of faith, hope, or submission in followers is the mark of leaders everywhere.

Another element in the leadership of Jesus that is found in other leaders was his ability to gather up the teachings of the rabbis, the religious ideas of the people, the theoretical principles controlling the sound life, and fuse them into units that comprise the body of the moral law. Men have always known, for instance, about the law of gravity, but they could not define it, understand it, comprehend its nature, or really use it intelligently until Isaac Newton found his formula for it. Jesus did something very much like this for the moral law. This capacity for giving new emphasis, force, and clarity to ideas and notions and beliefs that are already held by people—though often held unknowingly or inarticulately—is the mark of the leader. It goes without saying that from this standpoint Jesus was the greatest leader of all time.

The third element is closely related to the other two. It is that a leader has a program—a plan, a way to meet difficulties, a solution to a problem. He is going somewhere; he is leading in the direction of the Promised Land. Christ's program is summed up with infinite concreteness in the Beatitudes, the parables, and the Lord's Prayer—and also in the pattern of his own life, from beginning to end.

*   *   *

The fundamental trait of all leaders, great or small, is a true and intimate knowledge of their people. This is as obvious as the statement that a musician knows music, or an engineer knows mechanics, or a botanist knows plants. However, the leader's human subject matter is more unfathomable or mysterious than are the data of the physicist or the mathematician. Near the end of his life, Prime Minister Gladstone said that politicians were the most mysterious class in the human race. I am suggesting that politicians are very much like other people, and that human beings are the most mysterious data with which any scientist deals.

One reason why there is something of mystery that hedges about a human as contrasted with a mineral or vegetable subject is that a human can act as well as be acted upon. Or he can act not only in a greater variety of ways, but in more unpredictable ways, than does a non-human subject. But it is primarily because a human being can say "yes" or "no" to a leader's proposal, that a leader must know his follower, and the symbol, or issue, or plan that will win his consent, even before he can know his program. For he can not lead, no matter how wise or important his plan, if he does not have followers. A person with an idiotic plan and a controlling number of followers is still a leader, but an individual with even a great constructive program but no adherents is not a leader. He may be a voice crying in the wilderness, or a great professor or a creative thinker, but he is no leader.

Edmund Burke, at one point, said that "virtue and wisdom" were all the attributes that a leader needed. At another time he said that there was need for a leader with "not only a disposition to preserve but also the ability to improve." Although both of these statements are incontestably true, yet they are general. Here, I think I may go farther in pointing out the something that all leaders have in common. I think it is possible to identify traits of leadership—traits that are likely to be present in varying degrees, and regardless of the level on which the situation develops. (I am speaking of leadership in the Western world and, more particularly, in our own democratic process.) Some of these traits that are common to all situations and movements are: the ability to know people as a Toscanini intuitively knows music, to gauge the drift of public sentiment, to be articulate in a way that will cause a controlling number of people among the potential followers to inwardly think, "That's me—those are my sentiments"; the possession of a golden voice that matches and supplements the gold, or the complementary metal, in the followers; the ability to see through to the very pith and marrow of an argument or a problem; the faculty of picking the kernel of wheat from a mountain of chaff, and holding it up for all to see; a certain boldness, a firm and determined will—one that doesn't know defeat; initiative—the ability to make decisions on the instant; a sense of timing; a plan or program that seems to point to a better day, or, as Lord Bryce said, "that higher kind of wisdom which looks all around and looks forward too"; the ability to energize—to charge people with new life; the ability to lead, retreat, or stand pat as the situation develops.

One of the most important elements in leadership is the desire of the people to be led. Although this desire to be led is a constant, the quality and the intensity of this basic drive is a varying thing, depending both on the nature of the people and on the spirit of the times. The leader, in any case, is a symbol—a flag with a voice. Whether or not the voice is a whisper or a shout will depend upon a particular situation. This idea is clearly shown by the briefest glance at the very recent history of the institution of Monarchy. Here, in eras of comparative peace and prosperity, the qualifications of the leader (the king) are of secondary importance. But war and economic depression cause a tension in the minds of a people; and they usually want a dynamic leader under those circumstances. The selection of the non-hereditary leader depends on the confidence that he can inspire.

How strong the desire to be led is, depends on how comfortable the people are. They want powerful leadership when the situation that confronts them cannot be handled by their individual efforts; moreover, initiative, and the willingness to assume responsibility and make decisions, are qualities not frequently found in the general run of men; and yet there must be someone to lead the way. One thinks of a gigantic man sitting in the sun, fishing, eating, sleeping, dreaming, when he has a mind to. All the creature comforts are his. He may think some time he will be led to greener pastures, but this one is very nice, thank you. So he will just sit. The leader he wants is a politician who is determined to maintain the status quo. But the situation changes overnight.

The great man's sleeping and waking hours are sorely troubled. There are few fish and his tackle is worn out. There is not enough food and his shelter does not protect him from the wind and rain. There is danger of attack from the tribe across the way. Now he does not like the status quo. He wants leadership.

Napoleon was wrong when he declared that every soldier had a marshal's baton in his knapsack. William Allen White has said that "only one man in ten will freely take responsibility and stand the gaff of the consequences.... They [our public officials] think that they want leadership but they are scared of it." Undoubtedly Ford spoke for more than automobile plant employees when he expressed the opinion that his workers want routine work day after day, something that does not require initiative, thinking, or the necessity of making a decision. The strength of dictators in much of the world today supports this idea—as it relates to people without thorough training in self-government.

My best illustration of the value of the leader depending on the enthusiasm of the group for leadership is about the experiences of a highly intelligent person interested in finding support for refugees. This person first campaigned among the people in a small inland town on Long Island. He spoke to both groups and individuals, and everywhere he met dark, suspicious and hostile attitudes. A month later he started explaining his idea in a near-by town on the seaboard. Again he spoke to groups and to private individuals. But here the response was enthusiastic, eager and abundant. In the first place he felt chilled and frustrated. In the second place he was a different person. His power that had atrophied came to life, and became ten times the power it had been. He was a hundred times more effective. He accomplished a great social project that he had scarcely permitted himself to dream about under the conditions that had confronted him at first. Here the mass made the leader; the leader did not make the mass.

Of course the leader was indispensable too. There was a problem, and although everyone had some sort of idea about what America could do for deserving refugees, yet it took someone with a seeing eye, true initiative, a feasible plan, and an articulate voice to start action. The leader dramatized the plan so that it became meaningful to people that could not quite think of it before. Probably it is truest to say that in leadership there are both the leader and the led. Like the bow and arrow, one without the other is valueless.

*   *   *

Leadership is the crux of the governing process. A state, a business, or a movement is described by the leader it supports. This choice of leaders is invariably the most significant thing a person or a people do. For the choice not only sets the direction a state will go, but may determine the greater question of survival or death. And the tragic case of Hitler's rise to leadership and the result of a people's desire to be led illustrates the point that the qualities inspiring confidence in a people are not necessarily qualities of social value. In Hitler's case they are the lowest drives or qualities known to man, not excepting the uncivilized.

The leader himself must know people as individuals; he must be able to size them up and to estimate unfailingly their loyalty (a minister's loyalty to the throne may be worth more than his talents), their capacity in relation to a probable position or situation, and their value to the leader and the movement. This ability to pick the right man for the place is paramount for all leaders. To err at this point may be fatal to the cause, and the more people involved in the situation, the more certain is the fatality. The Colonel Sundlos and Quislings helped the Germans take Norway. The Norwegian leadership that did not know the traitorous intent of its officers in key positions lost their country.

Senator Josh Lee once said in a peaceful campaign that "some people like red birds and some people like blue birds, and I give red birds to those who like red birds and blue birds to those who like blue birds." This may be a formula for a politician but not for a leader. A leader is important when the people do not want either red birds or blue birds, when they do not know which they want or what the solution to their problem is. They want a leader because they want a plan of *action*, a program. In 1920, 1924, and 1928, the people wanted to let well enough alone; but in 1932 they wanted a leader who would do something.

And they got a leader! The briefest glance at Franklin D. Roosevelt's place in our political process since 1933 will tell us something about leadership in a free society. The President took office on March 4. He validated the fact that the banks were closed by declaring a banking holiday the next day. He summoned the Seventy-third Congress to meet in extraordinary session on March 9 at noon. It was in session one hundred days lacking a few hours, and during this time it enacted more momentous legislation than any of the congresses that preceded it in our history. Within a brief half hour after its opening, the House received a message from the President asking for emergency banking legislation. The Banking and Gold Control Bill was passed by the House, passed by the Senate, and signed by the President on this same March 9. Public Law No. 2, an Act to Maintain the Credit of the United States Government, was passed by the House on March 11 (the Presidential Message had been received the day before), passed by the Senate on March 15, the conference report accepted by both the House and Senate on March 16, and approved by the President on March 20. The President's message on 3.2 beer was delivered on March 13; the measure was passed by the House on the 14th, the Senate on the 16th, and signed by the President on the 22nd. The Agricultural Recovery legislation, the Reforestation Corps measure, the Industrial Recovery and Control bill, the Railroad Reorganization measure, the Unemployment Relief bill, and the other six measures that made up the first part of the recovery program of the Roosevelt administration were all passed with a celerity extraordinary to one who has studied the checks and balances found in our fundamental law or who had observed the progress of legislation under Mr. Roosevelt's predecessor.

There are various causes for the unparalleled speed with which those bills were passed, but only the two main ones concern us here. First, action was the demand of the hour. The public, all the publics, wanted something done; but the public didn't know what. Neither did Congress. But the President did know, and his orders were obeyed with alacrity—carrying them out was a patriotic duty, or so it seemed to nearly everyone. Roosevelt's voice at this time was comforting, as a mother's voice is comforting to a child in the dark. Roosevelt's disarming frankness, his apparent willingness to take both Congress and the public into his confidence, his suggestion that he was using every effort to get the facts, and acting as wisely as it was possible for him to act became the nation's symbol of hope and security. In May 1933, in speaking over the radio on what his administration was doing, he said, "I do not deny that we may make mistakes of procedure as we carry out the policy. I have no expectation of making a hit every time I come to bat." These words were spoken in a language that the people understood—it is native American. The leader does not know everything; he is doing his best. He does not say that he is other than mortal, or that the people are less than free agents, able to support or reject. The President's prestige has varied since that time, and the prestige of his program, especially specific parts of it, has varied even more. But in the November 1934 election the voice of Roosevelt was the voice of America. On the second day following the election, the *New York Times* editorially stated, "No previous President halfway through his term ever won such an overwhelming popular endorsement as Mr. Roosevelt received on Tuesday. . . . The President's personality dominated the whole campaign. It was as if he were present at every polling place. The whole constituted an individual triumph for the President such as never came to any of his predecessors, whether in peacetime or in war."

In June before the election the President, in one of his many nationwide broadcasts, said, "Among our objectives I place the security of the men, women, and children of the nation first." This idea is strengthened in people's minds not only by the legislation enacted during this administration but by the unprecedented action of a President speaking to the voters of the nation after elections as well as before. He once said that the most vital and rare ability in a President (political leader) was to "arouse in the citizenship an active interest—a willingness to reassume its share of responsibility for the nation's progress." And at the end of his first year in office he counted the work that he had done in this direction—arousing the people's interest in their government—his greatest contribution to the public welfare.

Two days after the Germans invaded Holland and Belgium May 14, 1940, Roosevelt made an emergency address to Congress and the nation. Both the ruthlessness and the effectiveness of the Nazis in bringing violent death and destruction to neutral countries and the traitorous actions of some of the people living in them brought home at last to the American people the awfulness of the German threat to world peace and American security. Roosevelt characterized the situation in a flash. He expressed the moral indignation of our more sensitive people. He asked Congress for a billion dollars for defense. He asked for 50,000 planes a year. He said, "Congress and the Chief Executive constitute a team where the defense of the land is concerned." When he had finished speaking, it was as though a mighty shout had gone up everywhere—saying, "Bravo! Bravo!" Or, "The President is right! It is true! So shall it be!"

Immediately Kaltenborn, a radio commentator, and Dorothy Thompson, a columnist, declared that the Republicans should not hold their convention for nominating a President this year, but should unite with the Democrats in reelecting Roosevelt. There was but one vote in the House against the defense appropriation measure, and the Senate was unanimous in its favor. A few days later the Gallup Poll reported 86 per cent of the people favoring President Roosevelt's defense program and 14 per cent opposing it.

Before I go on I must say that I fully realize the criticism that will come to me for selecting Roosevelt as the chief example of a leader in my discussion of leadership in America today. He has a singular faculty for inspiring the extremes in hatred and adoration—few voters are indifferent to him. (He is a good hater himself, and has intense personal loyalties.) To mention his name to some people is to cause them to immediately dribble bile. The foreign dictators count him their chief enemy. People of the President's own social class, many wealthy individuals with their stake in the old arrangements and in stocks and bonds, and those who are disturbed by change, count him a traitor. Their chief accusation is that he stirs up the poor against the rich. They hold the maxim, "Better let sleeping dogs lie." And then he is hated because he stands out, has opinions, and is usually the master of the situation. And there are many reasonable and intelligent people who strongly oppose Roosevelt because they think that his fiscal or other policies are unwise and, if continued, will undermine our institutions.*

* The Honorable T. Henry Walnut, a distinguished member of the Philadelphia Bar, and outstanding as a gentleman and citizen and public servant, read this section of my manuscript on Roosevelt. I had asked Mr. Walnut's opinion because he knows politics, has a very keen mind, and is a Republican. In reply he wrote in part:

"If I were writing an essay on the same subject—although I do not profess to be a Roosevelt advocate—I could still adopt almost all of your discussion. Where I could diverge from you would be in conceiving of the President as the leader of a great political party, and I would place more emphasis on the political expediency of his acts than upon any suggestion that they could be attributed to personal conviction. I probably would portray him as first, last and all the time a politician who overlooks no bets but who has sufficient capacity to comprehend the significance of his speech relative to the stabbing in the back, as well as the significance of a $1200 job or an $8.00 relief check."

Of course, Roosevelt is a politician—a great politician. Politicians are as indispensable to our democracy as doctors are to our hospitals or as engineers to our railroads. If all of the politicians, doctors, and engineers

But the action of the Democratic Convention in 1940 that overwhelmingly nominated him on the first ballot—and for a third term—is more than a straw in the wind. This unprecedented action's significance is increased by the fact that the nominee made no visible effort to get votes. That he was nominated for a third term is proof that the delegates believe him indispensable to their success in November.

I hope my readers will realize that in a discussion of leadership it is inevitable that I discuss Roosevelt for, whether we like it or not, he is the greatest leader of our day. And I must further say that I have not attempted a biography, but merely a brief examination of those of the President's qualities that partially explain his capacity to lead.

* * *

It is difficult to single out any one trait to the exclusion of several others and say, for example, that Roosevelt is a leader because of the magic and compelling appeal of his voice, or that he has initiative, or a rare sense of timing—the faculty of acting and speaking just at the precise psychological moment; or that because of his intimate knowledge of the mind of the American public he could speak what they most wanted to hear, but did not know it until they heard it spoken; or that he has a certain boldness, a willingness to break with tradition in order to meet the

---

were killed tonight, we should necessarily begin preparing men for these roles tomorrow. However, each of these three roles requires specialized skills and techniques, and we should doubtless experience much confusion and great waste in the interim. And finally when our new politicians, doctors, and engineers did appear we should probably find that they were inferior to the ones that we had destroyed. They would certainly be inferior at first and for some time in the future. Nor does Carl Sandburg's recent biography let us forget that our greatest hero—Abraham Lincoln—was also our greatest President and our greatest politician.

problem of the hour; or that he has the ability to make decisions on the instant; or that he knew what to do—that he saw a way out of the difficulties; or that he energized the people—charged them with new life. Roosevelt has all these qualities and he uses all of them. The end product of his capacity as a leader is the fact that when he first became President he found the people afraid and troubled in mind and spirit, and he gave them a great Hope in place of a Great Fear.

I have not mentioned the Roosevelt smile, but it is a real factor. Methods of communication through the radio and the printing press, and visibility through the talking motion picture have been improved to so great a degree that the people in Oshkosh or Perth Amboy may have a clearer picture of the man in the White House than they have of the alderman in their own third ward. Furthermore, the leader in the White House awakens response in them—and that is not often true of the alderman in the third ward. And if the city is big enough its third ward has a ward leader. But he is not a leader in the sense that he deals in opinions and ideas; he is rather a pillar in a stationary machine. The wheels of the machine revolve but the machine is not going anywhere. It attempts to satisfy personal needs, and rests its case on personal service and personal attention. It is not concerned with public discussion; opinions vary when it comes to ideas, but a loaf of bread is a loaf of bread to anyone that is hungry. A leader like Roosevelt is concerned with public purposes—treating all people similarly situated alike. Therefore he can have a program and discuss it; not so one who is concerned with favorites, individuals as individuals; no program would explain why one culprit is freed but not another.

But in addition to the Roosevelt smile and spiritual hand-clasp, there have been more goods and services delivered by the New Deal than any ward leader had ever dreamed possible; more jobs and relief checks disbursed than any little politician ever had at his disposal. (However, I do not mean to suggest that the voters on relief are any less free in marking their ballots than are school teachers, shoe clerks, or business men. It happens that the most doubtful voters in the electorate are the farmers, and they are the ones who have received the most federal monies.) But there is political wisdom in this figure of speech of Will Rogers': "As powerful as a Democrat with a Treasury behind him." I mention this aspect of the Roosevelt leadership because it is part of the smile—a smile that is heart-warming in itself, and that tells of help and benefactions to come.

*   *   *

Three of the most powerful leaders in the world today have the three most powerful voices. Hitler is one of the three—his voice is coarsest, but a proper voice for a people whose language is guttural, and whose tendencies, some-time or other, go to all of the extremes. Winston Churchill's voice is rich and sardonic, rhythmic, effortless, measured, as great English literature is measured. Franklin Roosevelt's voice is that of an American thoroughbred who speaks our common language with ease, geniality, and conviction. His voice is rich and intimate, and even though 3,000 miles intervene, it is as though he were in the room with you.

Borah once said that he waited and read Roosevelt's speeches, but he did not listen to them. If he listened, he was sure to believe, but if he read the message, he could make up his own mind. I know a Jewish refugee from

Germany, a man with a finely trained legal mind. He told me that he knew people in Germany who were bitterly and unutterably opposed to Hitler and all his works, but hearing Der Führer speak they found themselves agreeing with him—and this to their own amazement. These instances indicate that a voice does not appeal to the reason alone, but appeals to the total being. In a world being destroyed by war one imagines that it is the liver or the bowels—it can't be the brain—that is calling the turn.

The voice, whether an instrument of reason or an implement for non-rational appeals, is likely to be found in the leader's equipment. I think it is certain to be found in the arsenal of the leader who has a program or who appeals to ideas. It is less likely to be found among the attributes of the kind of leader who deals with people privately—face-to-face contacts, either because his group is small, as in a ward, or because he has an effective party organization. Murphy of Tammany Hall is an example of a powerful leader in a powerful party organization who in the words of E. M. Sait owed nothing to forensic ability, and who found a nod of the head sufficient for his purposes.

I think the significant point here is that a leader in public affairs appeals to two groups or to groups on varying levels. He has one appeal aimed at the masses, the people generally. He has a working arrangement or a different sort of appeal for the substantial economic entities in the electorate. A bank, for example, will not support a silver-tongued Bryan, a hate-fomenting Coughlin, or a stand-pat Senator John Doe because the first two speak eloquently and the latter in a mediocre fashion; but if the bank supports any of the three, it will be for reasons that have nothing to do with voice timbre or rhythm. This, however, is not true of the janitor who works in the bank. I can illustrate this matter by describing the campaign technique of the late Sol Levitan. Mr. Levitan had six times been elected to the office of state treasurer in Wisconsin. He was a man of great originality and color. He was unusually effective in speaking to the public. He lost office in the Republican landslide of 1938. In the summer of 1939—more than a year before the next election—he began his 1940 campaign by personally visiting the bankers in the seventy-one counties of Wisconsin. A week before he died, in February 1940, he told me that he had covered all the bankers save those in three counties. I asked why he called on the bankers instead of the members of the party organization. He replied that the party committeemen often did not know what it was all about, but that the bankers were important in their communities. And then he added, "You see, the bankers know me. They remember that during the times when I was in, I spread the state's money around in four hundred or more banks. I did not put it all in a few big ones." The moral is that Mr. Levitan was the humorous and lovable Uncle Sol to the people; and to the bankers he was the state treasurer who deposited the state monies in their banks. I present this bit of evidence better to explain my statement that a candidate, even though he may have a remarkably persuasive voice, may—in addition— have other methods of winning support.

In addition to his voice F. D. R. has a party organization and other organizations that cover the forty-eight states as a finely meshed net covers the sea. This organization of the Democratic Party, composed of 150,000 or more men and women, may be likened to a national sales organization with high-pressure salesmen in every neighborhood in the land. These party workers live (often they live and die) in the precinct or ward or township where they try to sell the Democratic ticket to their people. Party committeemen and workers are often so influential that millions of voters in a presidential campaign, and regardless of the candidate, vote the ticket because the organization asked them to. They have a general at the top to guide, inspire, and co-ordinate their efforts. He is the chairman of the national committee, and from 1932 to 1940 his name was James Farley. He and his office sent out 3,000,000 pieces of mail to the party workers in 1932. To describe our leader's victories at the polls without mentioning the party organization would be like telling about Pershing's conquests in the first world war and ignoring the infantrymen and officers in the A.E.F.

Roosevelt illustrates another characteristic often found in a leader. He usually says the things that are immediately pleasing and acceptable to the people. This may be a mark of intelligence and strength or it may indicate a weak will. However, politics is the science of the possible. A leader who does not know this fact is apt to be impotent or dangerous. A democratic leader cannot go too fast for the mass—he must have fifty-one per cent traveling along with him, or he will be turned out of power. (Hitler may continue to survive in a country governed by force even with so few as fifteen per cent going along, provided these fifteen per cent have rifles and the others have not. But democracy is different.)

This does not mean that a democratic leader cannot introduce a new idea—cannot place a new emphasis on an old value—cannot add to the people's knowledge and understanding. The valuable leader does all this, and he must do more too. He must prepare the minds of his followers for the new situation. The leader is a teacher, a professor of civics or citizenship. He sets the problem. He calls the turn. He makes clear what has been hazy. He clinches what has been doubtful. Or he may start people thinking on a different plane. Roosevelt's speeches are almost as varied as the needs of the moment. Examples of his addresses that are descriptive of each of the above general statements come to mind. His Chicago "quarantine" speech of October 5, 1937, directed public thinking along new channels. It prepared the people, in so far as one speech can prepare it, for events to come. It quickened the people's interest in foreign affairs. I quote: "When an epidemic of physical disease starts to spread, the community approves and joins in a quarantine of the patients in order to protect the health of the community against the spread of the disease." This precedent-breaking address was commented on by the *New York Times* in this fashion: "It is by no means certain . . . that the President's words can safely be interpreted as complete abandonment of the traditional policy of neutrality."

The quarantine speech is an example of the President's leading, and he is way out in front. He did not merely repeat what everyone knew, but he pointed the way. And here is another example of Roosevelt's amazing faculty for instantly speaking on the point. Italy declared war on the Allies, and immediately Roosevelt declared in a worldwide broadcast, "On this 10th day of June, 1940, the hand that held the dagger has struck it into the back of its neighbor." The President offered our full material aid to the Allied cause. (The "stab in the back" figure was played up by the newspapers, and although many intelligent people think it descriptive of the facts, yet it will probably alienate the support of great numbers of Italians in this country in the 1940 elections. It was not in the President's manuscript, but was inserted while speaking, because of the fervor of the moment. That the President used this telling phrase is a tribute to him as a man capable of honest moral indignation; but unfortunately his emotions were too much involved at that instant for him to exert his customary discretion. Later I point out that a leader must stand somewhere between the extremes. Roosevelt almost invariably does, except in the matter of his openly expressed opinions concerning European dictators.)

The leadership traits and situations about which I have written are, I think, clear to all. Roosevelt's power to comprehend exactly the forces that affect the mind of the people and to discern what they desire and will support is periodically evidenced by the Gallup and other polls. The point here is that Roosevelt may speak and you or I may think that he has spoken wisely or he is dead wrong—that he uttered words of wisdom or pernicious folly—but that mirror of democracy, the Gallup Poll, almost invariably reflects an upturn in the President's popularity after a speech. (One of the rare exceptions to this trend came at the time he advocated a change in the Supreme Court.) Ordinarily his ability here is uncanny. The public opinion poll is a barometer, just as an election is a barometer, only the former poll may give a more refined reading, and it does speak with the authority of numbers fifty or more times as often as does the election.

*   *   *

The question may now be asked—does the leader have a philosophy? Does he have a program? Does his program meet the needs of the people? There is no easy or sure answer to these questions. Public approval is an answer to public approval, but it does not necessarily indicate the public value of a leader's program.

Roosevelt has no philosophy in the sense that a Hitler has a philosophy of super-Aryanism. Neither does he have a definite panacea like the single tax, or the public ownership of utilities, or the Townsend plan, as a sure cure to all our ills. In 1932 he described himself in these words: "Nothing is more striking than the simple innocence of the men who insist, whenever an objective is present, on the prompt production of a patent scheme guaranteed to produce a result. Human endeavor is not so simple as that. Government includes the art of formulating a policy, and using the political technique to attain so much of that policy as will receive general support; persuading, leading, sacrificing, teaching always, because the greatest duty of a statesman is to educate."

I do not think that Roosevelt has any clear understanding of long-range objectives (so far as domestic affairs are concerned). Instead of a well-articulated plan, Roosevelt is best in sizing up events as they unfold, or in seeing them just before they unfold: his timing is better than his faculty for long-range planning. He has a philosophy, a pragmatic philosophy of doing what he can for the people here and now. He centers his attention on the next step—not the distant scene. And he often may be impatient about this next step, or he may think that it has been taken when a law has been passed. (Actually, a test of a law is in its enforcement.)

Some people think that Roosevelt has failed to "plan" adequately—that is their chief criticism of him. No one human is best in everything, however. Any farmer knows the problem of breeding for dual-purpose cattle. The cattle that are best for beef are not at the same time best for dairy purposes. When breeders try to get cattle that are best in both ways, they end by getting cattle that are not best in any way. It is this situation in human affairs that produces the specialist—and this is an era of specialists. Roosevelt, if he is a specialist at all, seems to be a specialist in common sense; and that is a useful commodity for a democratic leader to possess. Moreover, some of his shortcomings are the result of the situation in which we are living. No previous President has been confronted with a problem of the kind before us now, nor have any of Roosevelt's predecessors planned so much or devoted so much thought, energy, and men to planning. The varied nature of the facts, the necessities of the situation, call for the limited sort of planning that Roosevelt has been part of. But his interest in the American way, in personal freedom, is paramount, although he does not believe that the public's business should be conducted in a helter-skelter fashion. He thinks, and he is trying to get the public to see, that there is no incompatibility between efficient government and the democratic process. He, like Lincoln, has a great faith in the American way of life. As *Fortune* said: "Both in the furniture of his mind . . . and in the background of his training the President is a product of the American tradition. He is, to an extent which is almost inconceivable in a public man, the embodiment, the present expression, the complete resultant of his country's historical development." This faith, or this attitude toward life and the eternal verities, is bed-rock.

With the well-being of men, women, and children as his objective, he "plays by ear" and improvises as he goes along. Or, to change the figure, he is an opportunist with a slide-rule and a brain-trust. He meets difficulties as they arise, but he does not meet them empty-handed. No President has ever before so relied on experts from pertinent fields as Roosevelt. He has called men from universities, business, finance, labor, industry, and agriculture. He knows what he does not know, and at these points he brings in the man who knows. He is an eclectic, with scientists at hand to implement his ideas. Our situation is new and, as I have said, the President experiments; his progress can often be described as dynamic rather than consistent. He is an individualist and believes in free enterprise and profits. He believes, too, that government is here to prevent any force or combination of interests from interfering with these rights.

*　　*　　*

The real question is, How good are Roosevelt's ideas? Are they big enough and wise enough to provide an ambit within which America can prosper? On this great point experts disagree, but both experts and laymen know that the paramount problem in the United States (I am here not considering the major questions of morals and war) in 1940 is economic—the question of distribution and unemployment. Roosevelt probably does not know the answer to this problem, but he recognizes it as a great one, probably the greatest that has confronted our people since the Civil War. He believes (I think) that the answer will be found to this problem through the give and take of public discussion and the development of events in the years to come.

When Roosevelt came to power our national income was about 42 billion dollars a year; now it is 70 billions, more or less. This means that an advance has been made in the problem of bringing prosperity to America. Of course, how much of this advance is the result of Roosevelt and his policies I do not know. He reached power when we were at the bottom of an economic cycle. We have since been on the up-grade. On the other hand, we might have gone on downward. But, regardless of who gets the credit, there are still too few houses, clothes, and jobs for our people. We have surplus and shortage; we have abundance and scarcity; our problem is one of distribution, not production.

The question still is, What should be done? The Republicans say—to put the matter in simplest terms—that the governmental brakes on business should be loosened; business should be given the green light to go ahead. The most vocal businessmen seem to think that their idle plants and idle money stem from wrong governmental policies and a hostile governmental attitude. Those who generally agree with the New Deal policies say that this idleness is caused from a lack of customers. And there are too few customers because of a faulty distribution of the national income.

At the other extreme—or seemingly so at first glance—are those who want the government to go farther. These men feel that "the rhythm of the nineteenth century can not be recaptured," that basic far-reaching institutional changes are needed if the American system is to survive in the years to come.

Roosevelt, and partly by virtue of his place in our official government, stands in the middle ground. The fact that he holds public office, that he is the responsible head of the government, is an incontrovertible reason why he, or any other leader in power, must always stop short of what either, or any, extreme advocates.[1] Stalin could not go as far toward a Socialist Society as Trotsky wanted him to. Hitler has stopped some distance short of the recommendations of his most extreme partisans. His position is somewhere between the right- and left-wing Nazis. A man in a position of power cannot have the freedom that a man out of office naturally enjoys. An economic expert is footloose and free compared to one who is guiding the destiny of a people. The expert may express in a book theories that are all wrong and yet his book will not ruin the country. However, if a President and Congress write a page or two of laws that are all wrong, this public action might undermine the morale of a nation.

And then there is another angle. The President in our country is not the government. He is only one major part of it. Often his recommendations are accepted by Congress and the people. But that is because his proposals seem reasonable to the legislature and the public. If, however, instead of offering something that the legislative bodies are prepared for, he were to suggest some sharp departure from traditional American practice and thinking, his unexpected proposal, under normal conditions at least, would be rejected, even as his so-called court-packing plan was rejected. How well President Roosevelt understands this basic fact is indicated by ex-Congressman Amlie's story. Congressman Amlie and about forty other individuals keenly interested in seeing the federal government act more vigorously on a certain problem, called at the White House. President Roosevelt listened to the group's discussion of what they thought should be done. Finally, when they had finished, the President spoke substantially in these

words: "I agree with all that you have said. I wish that
there were more men like you in Congress. For if I were to
offer such a bill as you now suggest, it would never pass.
The Congress is not ready for such a measure." This reminds one again that a leader can do only those things that
he has prepared the country for, or that the people are
ready to accept. Mr. Merriam once said that a political
leader's power, or the power of any public official, was
like that of a cashier in a bank. The public may see the
bank official surrounded by great stacks of currency. It
may naively think that the money belongs to the cashier.
Actually, however, we know that the currency belongs to
the depositors—that only so long as the cashier handles it
according to the rules of the bank is he free to handle it at
all. If he appropriates it for his own private purposes, he is
liable to arrest. And if the political leader does not use the
public power in accord with the wishes of the public, his
days as leader are numbered.

Roosevelt, accordingly, takes a middle course (as does
the public pretty generally). In trying to achieve his goal,
his vision of a better world for men and women, he has
battled at times, strenuously and long; and at other times he
has gone fishing with boon companions. Again he may
stand merely as a symbol; at another time he might be the
umpire watching the various pressures playing upon him
and upon the government. Sometimes he may seem to be
completely absorbed with the problems of labor; then in a
flash he is trying to appease capital. His path is not a
straight line; it is often zig-zag, or even broken. At the
present moment the leader seems to have abandoned domestic policies and shifted his interest from domestic policies
and reforms and is devoting himself more exclusively to

foreign affairs. (But, then, Adolf Hitler and Winston Churchill are doing that too.)

* * *

As I have said, Roosevelt has great confidence in the American way of life, and American institutions. His purpose is to preserve and improve these institutions, and if corrective measures are needed to restore them, or any of them, to their original usefulness, then he will support the legislation necessary to bring about the desired reform. He thinks that a patch here or a subsidy there may be needed, and he tries to provide the patch or the subsidy, whether for labor, business, or agriculture, that will square with the facts. Sometimes he reaches wrong conclusions, and then, generally speaking, the purging effect of experience plus public discussion rids the system of the obnoxious legislation. When experience proves the legislation beneficial it is removed from partisan debate and accepted by everyone.

I can best describe Roosevelt's attitude toward his objective, by quoting in a footnote excerpts from his message of April 29, 1938, to Congress, that led to the action of that body in establishing the Temporary National Economic Council. Roosevelt wanted to improve the working of our competitive system by restoring competition and eliminating monopoly. He wanted to find out why our economic system has not been working at anything like full capacity. He wanted to know why more of our savings were not invested in the capital goods industry.[2]

The Temporary National Economic Committee was organized in less than two months after the President's message. I have just (1940) received word that within a few months there will be available some sixty volumes of hear-

ings and monographs, in addition to more than thirty research reports. The scope of the Committee's inquiries is
indicated by the partial list of studies I have placed in a
footnote.[3] (I believe that the economic materials and viewpoints that have been assembled will prove useful to those
of our leaders who are trying to do something about the
great problem of distribution and unemployment.)

But this leader is not clear and simple like the single note
coming from a barrel organ, or like Jello that is all of one
color. He does not live in an ivory tower, and he is not a
scholar—though, as I have said, he hires scholars, experts,
and technicians, and though he often goes far from the
madding crowd in sea-going yachts. The fashion in the
experts changes more often than does the fashion in sailing
ships. It is only because of memory that one can understand that Hugh Johnson and Raymond Moley were once
associated with Mr. Roosevelt. And in those first experi-
menting days other specialists burned brightly for an hour
and then disappeared. In recent years, especially, the President has seemed to rely more on hunches, more on working
by rule of thumb and insights than on patiently waiting
for the findings of experts. Probably he himself is the best
expert on some questions, and on other problems the best
solution cannot be established by scientific method. As in
the case of the Supreme Court, Roosevelt too must make
some decisions that "depend on a judgment or intuition
more subtle than any articulate major premise." Although
his insights are often right and sometimes brilliant, yet he
errs too, as he did in 1937 when he materially reduced
public expenditures and a recession followed. (Surpris-
ingly enough, this attempt to balance the budget followed
the tremendous victory of 1936.) Although he is the great

experimenter, yet he has the disposition to profit by his mistakes. After the National Industrial Recovery Act of 1933 (described by President Roosevelt as "the most important and far-reaching ever enacted by the American Congress") was declared unconstitutional, the President established a Committee of Industrial Analysis to investigate the experience and results achieved under it.

Roosevelt is an enigma, but we do know that in temperament he is more the artist than the scientist. And he has the capacity to break off completely and relax. Probably this rare faculty enables him to survive as the responsible head of a great nation surrounded by a world in gigantic revolution. Certainly, if he could not disengage his own emotions from the spectacle of the world today he would expire.

Roosevelt has been more effective in dealing with the public and bureau chiefs and other people in the administration than he has in dealing with Congress. He has neglected to woo the congressmen. He has not played up to their vanity. He does not give Congress the idea when something important is accomplished that the credit belongs to them. In the old days, when the elder La Follette was alive, he would usually pick the state ticket—but he would consult with a number of people, and he would tell them that their opinion was enormously important. Roosevelt, however, does not always talk over bills in advance, with Congress; he sends them a message. His talk is with his chosen associates rather than with Congress or his official cabinet. Congress would like to be consulted more—their egos require attention. So do the egos of the public, and Roosevelt evidently feels that time is short, and so he puts it on the people—the masters of Congress. The President has more of the executive than the legislative training and mentality. Executives must act. Legislators confer and discuss and compromise. Roosevelt is more willing to accept a compromise from the legislature than he is to go over his plans with them.

During Roosevelt's first term Huey Long called on him for a showdown, but Farley—who was a third person present—said that Roosevelt was master of the situation all the time. And so it is with other people who call on the President. He meets people well, is very cordial and friendly, and he usually does much of the talking himself. In these personal conferences one is impressed by his apparent honesty and frankness. The other person gets the idea that Roosevelt is taking him into his confidence. He guides the conversation, and on some occasions people who come to see him about a particular question are not able to get a word in edgewise. You remember that you are talking to the President of the United States—and as you sit there, face to face, you are struck with the feeling that this man has a dignity commensurate with the office.

It is almost impossible for the American people ever to remember that Roosevelt is partially crippled by infantile paralysis, which struck him in the prime of life. The respect of the people, and Mr. Roosevelt's own stature, both come, in part, from the way in which he has triumphed over a blow that would have ended any career for a lesser man. Not only does he manage to live a normal life, but he almost reminds one of Shakespeare's exuberant line: "Fie upon this quiet life! I want work." Roosevelt's fund of energy has enabled him not only to act strenuously in strenuous times but to keep his health and buoyancy and good humor during more than seven years in an office which has been described as the most difficult job in the world.

He sees life as a game, partly like chess and partly like bridge—like chess because the pieces have varying powers as do political figures in real life, and much depends on one's ability to see the move ahead of the next move; like bridge in that there is an element of luck, and what happens depends on the other player and the cards as well as upon himself. He follows the rules, where there are rules; and when he wins it is partly because he has made his position invulnerable, and partly because he can, up to now, out-smart, outguess, and outmaneuver the opposition. Further-more, his values are in accord with the best American tradition. Instead of Hitler's idea of domination and sup-pression, contempt for individuals, the use of death or prison for critics, and the exaltation of the lie, Roosevelt relies on persuasion, he encourages the individual to par-ticipate in the leadership process, he counts the significance of the individual paramount, and he is loyal to truth and honor. While a Napoleon or a Hitler is motivated exclu-sively by a desire for power, Roosevelt is striving for values that are important to civilized people.

*   *   *

The great question about any leader revolves around his sense of values. There is always the situation in which the temporary advantage is in conflict with the more perma-nent future good. When should one accept a set-back for the sake of the cause, for the sake of the well-being and happiness of those who come after he has gone? The demo-cratic process is made out of a series of conflicts. There is the conflict of the present and the future—and the future cannot vote. There is a conflict between consumers and producers, and only the latter are effectively organized. Some people think there is a very serious conflict between Boss Hague, who denies civil liberties, and the democratic way of life as guaranteed by our bill of rights. There is a conflict between a boss like Pendergast, who takes a bribe, and the common good. There is a conflict between war and peace.

The point is, on which side of the conflict does the leader throw his weight and influence? This depends upon the temper of the people, on time and circumstance as well as upon the will of the leader. There are instances when Roosevelt has failed to act, yielding to pressure, against what must have been his better judgment as to what actually constitutes the common good. How future Presidents may act in similar situations is of course anyone's guess. But when one compares F. D. R. on this score with his more immediate predecessors, he passes, if not with flying colors, at least well in the vanguard. In judging the leadership of President Roosevelt, the situation in which he is found must be examined. He was elected President on the Democratic ticket. The Democratic Party has powerful members, some in Congress and some out of Congress, who are no more interested in some of Roosevelt's great social objectives than are Herbert Hoover and other people who want to bring back the world of 1929 ante. I think it is Mr. Villard who once bemoaned the fact that there is no one in the New Deal camp who has been able to electrify the country as Mr. Hitler has electrified Germany. I think the comparison ill advised and misleading. Hitler is dealing with Nazis, and Roosevelt is working with American citizens. The Germans obey, or else—the Americans have the great privilege of freely deciding what to do. A profound question of this sort—when to yield and when to remain adamant—does not permit of a brief answer; space does not permit a long one.

Listing the traits of leadership as I have done is apt to be misleading if one is led to think that every leader has these traits, or that any one leader has all of them. Nevertheless, these traits are real even though some men may have great eloquence and lack will power, or great charm and lack a knowledge of economic reality. Again, a man may be a great thinker and understand financial problems never dreamed of by a Bryan, and yet lack a knowledge of the temper of the people. A pertinent case is that of the late Senator Borah. He had true eloquence, a kind of honesty, a great knowledge of constitutional law, and he had much else; but tragically enough he lacked the ability to carry on to the end of a fight. In the midst of a battle, if it were long and tedious, he might turn to other matters. He might lead today, but tomorrow he might not be in the fight at all. He was often exceedingly persuasive at first, but his followers were apt to lose their confidence in him before the fight was ended. This was partly because he lacked staying power, and partly because he did not know how to cooperate with his colleagues who were working with him for a common goal. He did not know the importance of "the function of compromise. This is a function that is indispensable in a democracy." He was not a good parliamentarian—an attribute of leadership important to those in legislative bodies. He did not appreciate the importance of suggested amendments, of viewpoints other than his own. He might proclaim a reform in glittering generalities, but not keep interested in it long enough to see it put into statutory form.

A leader in the United States Senate must be a good parliamentarian, and that means that his mind must have resiliency. He must be able to take it as well as to give it; to follow as well as to lead. One single person cannot always lead. He cannot always be in the forefront of the battle, managing and planning the campaign. At some times and on some issues he will be lined up behind some other person who is leading the fight for supremacy. Professors specialize, and Senators do too. No brain is big enough to map out every major fight and to know clearly all the technicalities that are apt to be involved in carrying on various senatorial campaigns.

A leader in the Senate or elsewhere must clearly see the problem or the situation that needs to be changed. He must also think out a method of improvement. To know merely what is wrong is not enough; to lead effectively he must be able to nail a concrete solution to the problem on the reverse side of his complaint—and in preparing this solution he must consider the matter from every conceivable angle in order to be familiar with every possible objection that may be raised against him, so that in the midst of the fight no surprise attack will find him unprepared.

It is a truism to say that a leader in the Senate, or elsewhere, cannot lead unless he has followers—followers who are faithful and who will stick to the end. And, if we consider the leadership of Senator G. W. Norris, we find one who has earned the love and trust of his fellows, not because he has more leadership traits than other Senators, but, I think, first because of his ability to see an issue clearly, and usually to suggest a concrete method of improvement, and, more important still, because of his possession, to a superlative degree, of that great and rather rare trait—integrity.

Senator Norris could never agree with those who hold with Shakespeare's Edward:

> "But, for a kingdom, any oath may be broken,
> I'd break a thousand oaths to reign one year."

The record of this Senator's life shows that he would rather lose a fight than deceive his followers. His philosophy is based on the idea that if he loses the fight and yet retains the confidence of his followers, he has nevertheless increased the power of his leadership and prepared the day for the fight he will win. The idea that the end justifies the means is anathema to him, and this is a major reason why his leadership has survived for so many years.

The Honorable Dan Hoan is another leader whose character is sterling, and whose political sagacity is indicated, but only in part, by his record in successfully facing the ballots of Milwaukee's democracy fifteen times in thirty years (three times as a candidate for city attorney and twelve times as the mayoralty candidate). His victory has been all the greater because he is a Socialist and Milwaukee is not Socialist. In the election years that span the period (1910–40) when Milwaukee elected Hoan, they invariably elected a council that was more than half non-Socialist. So great was the confidence in Mayor Hoan that people who were not Socialists voted for Hoan the Socialist. To quote Mr. Richard E. Krug: "He had a peculiar mixture of aggressiveness and personal modesty which appealed not only to the average man but to the professional and successful business man. The best evidence of this almost universal appeal is his ability to consistently carry the 18th Ward of Milwaukee which consists of Milwaukee's 'gold coast' and the upper middle class families." They did this from

1910 until 1940, when some 12,000 citizens defeated Hoan
by voting for an amazing young man with curly hair and a
baritone voice.

Hoan is one of the foremost municipal leaders in the
United States. To describe his leadership means first of all
to consider his followers. His leadership is not the sort that
is spasmodically supported by followers who want to get
on the bandwagon; get the money, get the jobs. "We want
to get the stuff," describes some municipal followings, but
not Dan Hoan's. He is an excellent campaigner. He can get
down to the factory gates, give a short, hard-hitting talk
to the men before they go back to work. He can compete
with all the city noises and still get his idea over. And this
talking at factory gates is very important in Milwaukee.
But whether he is addressing an industrial group, a parent-
teachers' association meeting, or a nationality group, Mr.
Hoan can talk effectively about issues. Once he was explaining to a gathering of Milwaukee Greeks how he proposed to free Milwaukee from thirteen million dollars of
debt. He dramatized his talk with his hands. He held one
hand at a certain low level to show the money that had
been paid—seven million dollars. He used the other hand at
a higher level to show the debt. And then as his talk progressed, he counted the debt on his fingers. Then he came
to a point where the two hands would be level. This meant
that the debt was gone. One of the members of the audience said, "He makes us understand, whether we understand or not. We do understand."

This power of Mayor Hoan's to crystallize some latent
urge of a group into a definite objective and then to energize the group so that it will act is of great importance.
Hoan used skill and resourcefulness in directing the ener-

gies he had awakened into effective channels. He was the center of much activity that was meaningful. Moreover, he had vision that enabled him to look out beyond Milwaukee and to be concerned with what was happening in other parts of the state and the United States. "He picked up the dying League of Wisconsin Municipalities and breathed life into it, and became the president of the Great Lakes Harbor Association and made it an effective lobbying force." He also strengthened the American Municipal Association, and helped to organize the United States Conference of Mayors, which, during the depression, became a vital factor in helping Washington know the wants of the cities throughout the country.

He is, I think, a democratic statesman. He worked year in and year out to build up a democratic movement in Milwaukee. He thinks of leadership as a group process. He had a program, but it was not the work of any one man. Everyone had some say in building the program. When a platform was to be written, Hoan and six or seven hundred active workers in first the Socialist, and later the Farmer-Labor, Party of Milwaukee County would meet in a large auditorium with a big black-board. Hoan would ask, "What are your ideas?" Someone would mention his idea and it would be written on the board. This procedure would be followed amid the winnowing process of discussion until the first ideas of the group were up on the board for all to see. These statements would then be discussed some more, and finally all of those that had some general support would be written on a piece of paper. This first rough draft was then turned over to a platform committee for further study and deliberation. It was then reported back to the group, and when it was accepted by them, the party had a platform.

It was then presented for the people's acceptance. If the people did not recognize it as their program at once, an educational campaign began—or rather, that educational campaign in Milwaukee democracy is going on all the time; it is merely intensified during campaigns. Hoan got up on his hind legs and put the matter to them in a convincing fashion. (He believes in telling the voters at the right time; he uses facts, figures, and concrete illustrations in explaining what he is doing in his city and theirs.) He said that he was fought so bitterly that he had to take this way to keep the people informed. He is as common and homely and honest as an urban Abe Lincoln. He lacks Lincoln's wit and humor, and yet one of the most important elements in his platform success is his ability to enliven the more serious moments with a sudden bit of humor or by a smart saying or a caricature directed against his opponents. He speaks with vigor and his discussions are lectures about economic and political questions that citizens should know. He refuses to campaign on the issue of cutting taxes. He would argue that the tax dollar buys the citizen more than does any other dollar he spends. He courageously and persistently advocated the building up of public services and devoted much nervous energy to educating the voters on the incontestable, but rarely accepted idea that these objectives could not be obtained without adequate tax support.

Of course the value of this sort of speech would depend on the electorate. He has been preparing the electorate for many years; yet in 1940 it seems that a controlling number of the voters wanted something different. Good government, after all, may not have the appeal in a restless world that, say, Ann Sheridan's leg has. The sober Hoan was defeated in 1940 by a candidate who put on a show, and the figures in it differed only in degree from those Hollywood use; but they were altogether different from the ones that Hoan had employed in appealing to the voter.

Hoan is not only unselfish, but his long leadership has been based on the idea that everyone should be a leader. That means that everyone should participate in reaching conclusions. Hoan gives the group, the movement, much credit for what has been accomplished in Milwaukee. He gives the method of discussion all the credit. He would get civic and service groups to elect their own delegates—about fifty-four of them—to an advisory committee. This mayor's advisory committee would regularly meet once a month and there would be special meetings, in addition. At these meetings with the mayor, municipal questions would be discussed before the official government acted on them.

Mayor Hoan believes that this is the crux of the Milwaukee plan; and credit for all the first prizes and medals and ribbons that the city's administration has won stems from this device of general and group discussion. The mayor once told me, "If our philosophy is great, we need a movement like this. Put seven hundred to one thousand people in a room and talk about our objectives, our program. The people who can think best will be the ones whose words and ideas will stand out above the rest. Our government has been more democratic than anything else in this country."

To lead in a movement like this one, one must be a thinker and an organizer. Dan Hoan is both. In addition to being a thinker and having great stores of nervous and physical energy, Mr. Hoan knows human nature and is honest.

To know human nature is to be able to pick the right man for the right place. Some people fit and some do not fit.

The leader must select those that do. Some of Dan Hoan's strength has lain in the fact that he can often do this, and he can often express gratitude to his associates for their part in the movement. However, it seems that whenever one finds a champion of the people like Hoan or the late Senator La Follette he has a person who, possibly by the very nature of things, is jealous of his place in the sun. Most men in this sort of position do not relish the idea of hearing another voice in the show that is as big as their own.

Long ago, when Gifford Pinchot was serving his first term as Governor of Pennsylvania, I heard this story in the City Hall at Philadelphia. Governor Pinchot, according to the story, had died and gone to heaven. The first day St. Peter asked the Governor what he thought of the place. Mr. Pinchot said that he would look around first and then answer. A few days later the Governor came to St. Peter with a list of comments and suggestions. As he handed his document over, he asked St. Peter what he thought God would think of it. St. Peter read the comments and then he said, "These ideas are all right, but there is one here that I do not think God would like." "Which one is that?" asked the gentleman from Pennsylvania. "The one where you suggest that God be Vice-President," St. Peter replied.

This story is descriptive, but it may also be misleading. If a man is primarily concerned with the common good, with the welfare of the people as a whole instead of with an organized minority, he must do a lot of advertising to put his program over. He cannot do this advertising unless he stands out himself, and dramatizes this program. This means that the opposition will call him "The Great I Am." These accusations have been made concerning Mayor Hoan; and some observers feel that he surrounded himself only with second-rate men. But he could never have done his great work as administrator without having made many good appointments, without having used many men of outstanding ability.

*   *   *

About midnight of June 27th Wendell L. Willkie was nominated. For many hours and several days before this sixth ballot was completed, I had been listening to the words of the Republican orators; and all I had heard had been words, words, words. Probably these pompous and make-believe sentences and paragraphs and speeches meant most to the persons who uttered them. They dealt only in extremes and superlatives, and I, for one, regretted that I could not hear one—just one—shortcoming admitted in the Republican record, or one idea held by the Democratic leader that time had proved to be of value. But we are not mature or wise enough yet to have candor in the speeches at a National Convention. And then, suddenly and magically, everything changed—I heard Willkie's rich, leisurely, full-toned voice saying: "I am overwhelmed, I am deeply grateful—and now I want to join my family." It was refreshing to hear words that meant exactly what they said, and said what a reasonable person would naturally say at a time like that. The nominee's words cleared the air, and I felt good, as I have felt good when the sun comes out after gloom.

Mr. Willkie has never been elected to public office,[4] but no politician can show him how to talk to the public. I was struck by the same idea a few days earlier when I saw close-ups of the leading Republican candidates in a movie short. Here Willkie was the one that looked like a man—he seemed strong and virile, he was refreshingly informal in appearance, as though he had been caught by the lens just as he is in everyday life. He said: "I have no campaign headquarters. My campaign headquarters are under my hat." He seemed human and real and capable. As you looked, you thought of the Commonwealth and Southern Corporation and were not surprised that this man was its president. He looked like a resourceful person. He looked like a leader.

When Wendell Willkie spoke to the delegates at the convention on Friday afternoon, he again proved that he knew what to say and what to leave unsaid. First of all he paid a handsome and fitting tribute to Joe Martin, the chairman of the convention. Next he said he was an absolutely free man. Third, he expressed his great appreciation to the convention that had nominated him. He spoke of his devotion to the cause the delegates had asked him to lead. He then said, "And as your nominee I expect to conduct a crusading, aggressive, fighting campaign to bring unity to America, to bring the unity of labor and capital, agriculture and manufacture, farmer and worker, and all classes to this great cause of the preservation of freedom." Of course, everyone wants unity, and even those who feel that we have unity now, cannot object to a candidate's saying unity is his goal. He then identified himself as at one time or another having belonged to each of the groups he had just mentioned, and since these groups are general, they just about include everyone—and to have everyone think that he is "one of us" is especially nice for a man looking for votes. He spoke for a strong defense against dictators—and the Gallup Poll shows that this is what the American people want. Finally he said that it was only forty-eight days ago that he had begun talking to the American people about the doctrine of unity and the destiny of America, and the convention's action shows how appealing this simple doctrine is to the American people.

All of this speech followed the pattern of politics as it has been laid down by political speakers from the first. Willkie's tactics are the same. It is his strategy that is different. Whether or not his nomination was the natural upsurging will of the people's delegates in picking a leader, or an example of the higher strategy in seeing people who count at the right time, there can be no doubt that the nominee is living this very hour—and that he is of this day and tomorrow. Everything about his campaign, and regardless of all other considerations, smacks of the present moment. It is a blitzkrieg in politics. Old conventions, customary tactics, and political values thought to be indispensable to a candidate were either violated or forgotten. Somehow the delegates got the idea that this is no ordinary campaign, that a Taft or a Dewey might be all right in normal times, but they were not good enough for today. Today the situation required a leader—and the delegates got one.

He has a charm that draws people to him. He has a political sense—a flair for people and the immediate situation. He is exceedingly contemporaneous. He can speak with authority because he has achieved a high place in industry and finance. He is a symbol of Big Business, and to some that may be an asset in these times: there is a feeling that a more effective cooperation of government and business is needed to restore prosperity to America. His managers, however, are not relying on this. As I have said elsewhere, they are attempting to emphasize his "plain folks" aspect and diminish the background and picture that identifies him as the president of the Commonwealth and Southern Corporation. To put a utility president in the White House would shat-

ter a precedent as old as the third-term tradition. He is
articulate and speaks in the common idiom. Right after
Willkie's nomination, someone mentioned Roosevelt as the
probable choice of the Democrats. The Republican candidate cracked back: "Bring him out. I want to lick the
champ." His is a calm voice in a world again filled with
confusion and fear. There is a big job ahead and he seems
strong enough and wise enough to take a hand in doing it.

Mr. Willkie left the Democratic Party because the leader
of that party persuaded the Congress of the United States
to do something that Mr. Willkie did not want to see
done. This devastating thing that made a Republican out
of Mr. Willkie may have had something to do with the
mounting public debt, the spending program of the Democratic administration, the going off the gold standard,
the failure of Roosevelt to balance the budget, the failure of the Democrats as industrial organizers, or their
failure to meet adequately the unemployment problem; or
it may have had something to do with the objectives that
Mr. Willkie has mentioned in his recent speeches and writings; but, if it did, these matters were thought of later. The
crucial and overt thing that made a Republican out of Mr.
Willkie was the T.V.A. experiment in the Tennessee Val-
ley, an experiment of tremendous scope in the creation and
sale—at a lower rate—of electric power. Already it supplies
electricity to millions who had never been able to use it
before. And, of course, it competes with private utility
companies and has forced a reduction of their rates in this
area. No private utility likes this sort of thing. Nor did
Mr. Willkie, who was then president of a utility that was
in the center of the fight against the T.V.A. He re-
nounced the Democratic Party and became a Republican.

The question is really bigger than a power question. It goes right to the heart of modern government.

And regardless of the primary concern that our people feel and will feel about the European war now and on election day, November 5, 1940, this basic question—What shall the government do for the people, and what shall it leave undone and solely to private initiative?—will be in the background of the public mind, and it may be the controlling factor.

There are surface similarities common to both candidates, genial smiles, buoyant personalities, positive and dynamic characters, and the ability to stamp the public mind with a pungent phrase. Both candidates have a flair for people, and they know how to present politics as theatre. I sometimes wonder if Willkie has in him the capacity for growth, for rising to the greatness demanded of a man in the position to which he aspires. His smile, which is so unmistakably boyish, makes one wonder if he will ever be capable of genuine dignity and of experiencing that Weltschmerz that must overwhelm the sensitive person in this critical and agonizing age.

But there are real differences in these men. One is typical of business, although possessed of the higher business outlook; the other is typical of the public servant or politician, but he is an enlightened politician, and probably the most skillful one that has come down the road since Abraham Lincoln campaigned for votes. A few months before the Republican Convention met, Mr. Willkie wrote: "The essence of a great political platform remains always unwritten; it must nevertheless be related as well as possible to contemporary problems and events." The people will "give their vote to men. They vote for the man who, in their opinion, will not let them down."

He then presents the following petition as a foundation for a political platform for recovery.

"Before the political platforms are written, we, the people, have a declaration and a petition to make.

"In the decade beginning 1930 you have told us that our day is finished, that we can grow no more, and that the future cannot be the equal of the past. But we, the people, do not believe this, and we say to you: give up this vested interest that you have in depression, open your eyes to the future, help us to build a New World.

"In this decade you have separated 'business' and 'industry' from the ordinary lives of the people and have applied against them a philosophy of hate and mistrust, but we, the people, say: business and industry are part of our daily lives; in hurting them you hurt us. Therefore abandon this attitude of hate and set our enterprises free.

"In this decade you have undertaken vast new obligations, which we support. But because you have not applied to these obligations the ordinary standards of business judgment, you have lost our money by the billions and we, the people, say: give us a businesslike administration that will act as the steward of our prosperity; that will ensure the social progress that is now threatened, and will manage our affairs at least as intelligently as we manage our own enterprises.

"In this decade, under the banners of reform, you have usurped our sovereign power by curtailing the Bill of Rights, by short-circuiting the states, and by placing in the hands of a few men in executive commissions all the powers requisite to tyranny; and we, the people, say to you: we do not want monopolistic government, any more than we want monopolistic industry. Give us back the powers that our forefathers declared to be ours; liberate us to govern ourselves by law.

"Because you have concealed from us the amount of our real taxes, and because you have hidden from us the real nature of our expenditures, you have specifically usurped our power over the public monies, and we, the people, say: give us as much information concerning our government as we expect to get concerning our own enterprises, so that we may control the vast sums that it has become necessary to spend.

"You—the politicians of both parties—have muddled our foreign affairs with politics; with vague threats and furtive approvals; with wild fears and inconsistent acts; and we, the people, say: give us a foreign policy that we can trust and upon which we can build toward the future. We are against aggressors; we are for foreign trade; and we recognize that our own standard of living can be improved only by raising the standard of the other countries of the world.

*   *   *

"This declaration will not interest those who regard the United States as a laboratory for social experiments.

"It will not interest those who regard the United States as a free-lunch counter.

"It will certainly not interest those who regard the United States as a somewhat impoverished gold mine out of which they can still scrape a nugget or two for themselves.

"It will interest only those who think of the United States as their land—a land they know and love—a land that became rich through the industry, thrift, and enterprise

of its people, and will never regain its prosperity in any other way." [5]

W. L. W.

*   *   *

P. P. S.

After reading this petition the reader who is also a voter may examine F. D. R.'s message to Congress, excerpts of which are found below. He may then decide which of the candidates' statements most closely squares with his own ideas. Only in the case of F. D. R. the voter can judge the general results that have been achieved, and the failures suffered, in his two administrations. He can then try to imagine how much better Mr. Willkie might have done the job, or how much better he will do it in the future. Save that until Wendell L. Willkie is President, we cannot know what he will do. I can illustrate this last idea by a story I heard last April when I visited a town meeting in a rural community. In talking to a Mr. Osborne who had been supervisor for seventeen years, I said, "Here you can know your candidates—the community is so small." Mr. Osborne replied, "Well, we do know everyone here, but I can't even tell what my farm neighbor will do when he gets in office, until he gets in." "But," I objected, "you surely know whether your neighbor is honest or not?" "No, I don't know until he gets in office."

Of course, actually, some millions of voters knew before the convention met that they would vote for or against Roosevelt in 1940 if he were to head the Democratic ticket, and regardless of any other candidate. Millions too will vote one way or the other because they belong to the Democratic or Republican Party. Still other millions will be persuaded by party organizations to vote for the Democratic or Republican candidate. And then many voters, probably a controlling number, will follow the world and domestic situation as it unfolds in these momentous days and will vote for the candidate who seems to best define their own position, or rather the candidate who is most likely to provide the American with security, because this, too, is an election in which the voter is confronted by a great fear.

How much can one person ever know about another? The number of divorces granted in this country each year cannot be completely explained on the basis of ignorance in one person of the other's true character at the time of marriage, but I believe many of them can be. Some years ago I was living in a large borough in the East. I had not lived there long before I heard about the powerful rural boss, Jonathan Slade. Mr. Slade lived in a semirural borough, and the majority of people in the county lived in non-urban areas. My borough was the largest in the county and maintained a morning and an evening newspaper, both Republican. These newspapers often described Mr. Slade and his county board, of which he was the perennial chairman. But they never mentioned him save to lambaste, verbally lash, denounce and utterly reject him and all of his works. Their attacks were in editorials and news stories alike. All about Mr. Slade was black—black—black. Not a hint as to any strength that he might have. Not a suggestion as to how he maintained his position of supremacy in the political affairs of his borough and his county for nearly twenty years.

I became interested and visited Mr. Slade. I found he owned one of the two biggest gasoline stations in that part of the county. He looked old and wrinkled and gnarled, and he did not look pleased when I came upon him. But as I explained the purpose of my call, he relaxed, smiled, held out his two hands to take mine. After we had talked awhile he said, "I am as straight as a string, but the newspapers won't print that because they want my hide. I would have quit long ago—" And then he smiled and said, "I will never resign under fire. And I am Scotch clear through, and I am tight, as tight with the county's monies as I am with my own, and I am defending the rural people in this county against the city crowd." He went on to explain that the papers were against him because he tried to economize and wouldn't build a luxurious auditorium that a few of the ——— people wanted. And then, "Ask anybody who knows me. Don't take my word for anything. Here, let me show you something." He went to an old file, rummaged awhile among its contents, and produced a handful of letters; but the one of which he was proudest was a letter from the president of the biggest bank in the county. Its date told me that the letter had come right in the midst of a combined newspaper attack on the manner in which some road gravelling had been done. It follows verbatim, save for proper names.

Mr. Jonathan Slade,
—— —— ——.
Dear Jonathan:

In spite of the fire aimed at the ——— County Board from year to year, it must indeed be gratifying to you to be re-elected chairman term after term with no appreciable opposition. Especially must your past term in office have been a very trying one at times.

It gives me a great deal of pleasure to again be able to congratulate you in behalf of myself and the — — — group on your re-election as chairman of the board. Our best wishes for another outstanding successful administration.

— — —

President

I commented, "It must be nice to have a bank for a friend." He smiled and answered that truer words were never spoken.

After leaving Mr. Slade I called on his competitor in the gasoline business. He said, "J. S. is the best man I know, and if I have got to have someone else around here selling gas, I am glad it is old Jonathan." I talked to several voters at random, and they all agreed with what the gas dealer had said.

I walked away thinking that Mr. Slade knew the people of the small boroughs and rural areas and knew how to conserve their money. He knew the temper of the men on the board and was elected because these members thought he was doing a good job as their chairman. And the fact that the biggest bank was "for" him did not hurt one bit.

The moral of this is: what can the writer on leadership know about his subject? If a county leader is one thing as seen by the newspapers and something else as seen by a corporate interest like a bank, and still another when viewed by people living in a semirural borough, it is evident that the same subject is liable to many different interpretations. This problem in a rural county is comparatively simple; it is truly great when one attempts to portray a President who is still President.

So I will not say "finally"—for I know that much remains to be said about leadership—but for my concluding paragraph at this time I want to make this point. From time immemorial, until the national conventions of 1940 and beyond, biographers have written about the great lives— and the mean lives too; but whether or not the secret or the élan vital or the magic spark that sets one off from and above all his fellows—whether this "something" that makes the leader click in a given situation can be reduced to a verbal formula, is a question. Many facts, fancies, concrete events, and conversations can be recorded. But can the critical pressures, decisions, glances, and arrangements be known and reported? I think it was John Chipman Gray who once said that the rulers of society are undiscoverable. One might add that it is very difficult or impossible to state what the ruler has that enables him to rule. I know it would be forever interesting if we could hear some of Plutarch's subjects comment on the portraits that the great Plutarch drew of them. Would Romulus, Pericles, Marcus Cato, Alexander, or Caesar say, "That's it—that's how I did it— that explains me!" Might not the subject say rather, "Alas, all that Plutarch writes is true—but he has failed to mention the one crucial decision, or the fortunate meeting, or the help that I received from X, that was the turning point of my life, without which nothing else mattered, nothing else could matter!"

Even so great a leader as Winston Churchill who has associated for a lifetime with leaders cannot surely say what it is. From his own experience he knows much about the governing process, particularly as it relates to the English leaders and public. His problem then is one of language —the problem of using words that are rather rigid and static for describing the stream of life that is fluid and endlessly changing. One of Churchill's best descriptions is found in his comparison of George Nathaniel Curzon and Lloyd George. He said: "It was the very gift possessed by Lloyd George which the product of Eton and Balliol [Curzon] had always lacked—the one blessing denied him by his fairy god-mothers, the one without which all other gifts are so frightfully cheapened. He [Lloyd George] had the 'seeing eye.' He had that deep original instinct which peers through the surfaces of words and things—the vision which sees dimly but surely the other side of the brick wall or which follows the hunt to fields before the throng. Against this, industry, learning, scholarship, eloquence, social influence, wealth, reputation, an ordered mind, plenty of pluck, counted for less than nothing."

Here it is—but what is it? It is like standing on the edge of the sea pointing north-northeast and saying, "The ship went down about there." We do not know the exact spot, but we know the general direction in which to look. A story that I like is found in a biography of Zaharoff. An old wine merchant is on the point of death; and during his last few hours he is trying to tell his two sons the secret of his success as a vintner. He talks at length, and finally he smiles and remarks, "Wine can also be made from grapes, you know." The story illustrates the resourcefulness of one who has succeeded. And I think leaders have something of this quality in them too.

Probably the central idea is this. There is a situation, and the situation creates a leader. The group is faced with a problem, and the individual who can meet the problem or who can make the people feel that he can meet this problem and has a solution to their difficulties, is the leader. For example, Hitler had his program, his words and lung power and will in 1923, but he was a negligible influence in

Germany because the German people were able to earn a living and still had some morale.

But during the ten years between 1923–33 and after, Hitler, a genius in mass psychology, by means of propaganda and shrewdly devised demonstrations and riotings, devoted himself to undermining the moral resistance of the German people. The world-wide economic collapse proved an invaluable ally. This collapse, plus the German defeat in war, and various "wrongs" both real and imaginary were made by Hitler to seem to the Germans as wrongs deliberately put upon them by other people, as instances of unfair treatment. As Dr. Friedrich Roetter puts it: "Hitler created a spiritual depression in Germany." And he did actually "burn into the little man's soul the proud conviction that though a little worm, he is nevertheless part of a dragon."

As I have said before, the significant question to ask about a leader is this: To what does he appeal? Hitler appealed to the hate in the hearts of the Germans; he educated them in such a way as to make the hate motif supreme. By the time he came to power, the subjective depression had settled so squarely on the Germans that they, in their feeling of misery, resentment, and insecurity, were willing to forsake any traditional values they might have had, and follow Hitler. (A man who is drowning will grab at a straw; and a frightened or miserable voter will follow a strange leader.) Hitler came when the situation was "ripe"; but he himself had taken a hand in making the situation "ripe." He was and is the cause and effect. His human materials were fashioned to his design. Historical traditions, the weakness of the Republic, the lack of an ideology built around freedom and social responsibility, and economic conditions also helped fashion these materials, of course, along with Hitler and his Storm Troopers. The chief point is, however, that by 1933 the Germans lacked the moral courage to act, or to resist Hitler. This phase of what happened in Germany is most accurately described by Lawrence Hyde, a sociologist—who was writing about other matters when he put into words in his book, *The Learned Knife,* the steps whereby a society evolves, either upward or downward.

"Every situation with which the sociologist deals is the ultimate result of a series of small personal and domestic crises. The outer conditions which he investigates represent only the final expression of an infinite number of minor conflicts in the hearts of all sorts of individuals. What determines the circumstances, not only of a man and his family, but of a village, a city, and a nation, is an endless series of decisions, insignificant in themselves, but cumulatively of overpowering force. Such decisions are being made all the time by all kinds of people in all kinds of predicaments, and it is they that determine the final situation."

*   *   *

I know no more fitting conclusion for a discussion of leadership than these words of Theodore Roosevelt:

"It is not the critic who counts; not the man who points out how the strong man stumbled, or where the doer of deeds could have done them better. The credit belongs to the man who is actually in the arena; whose face is marred by dust and sweat and blood; who strives valiantly; who errs and comes short again and again; who knows the great enthusiasms, the great devotions, and spends himself in a worthy cause; who at the best knows in the end the triumphs of high achievement; and who at the worst, if he fails, at least fails while daring greatly; so that his place shall never be with those cold and timid souls who know neither defeat nor victory."

Emerson, I believe, said that an institution is but the lengthened shadow of one man. A leader, "miraculously magnified," is the country. The leader with his own and a synthetic magnetism given to him by the people through the unprecedented instruments of communication and a golden voice that speaks not only to the mind, but to the heart and soul of a people, is the teacher of citizenship without an equal in the whole land. His ideas, his attitude, his morals, his philosophy of life, the person that he is—all these place their imprints on millions of people. In Germany today there are millions of little Hitlers. In the United States today the leader, be it Roosevelt or Willkie—and even though conflicting ideas are encouraged in our free country—sets the example for everyone. His values and objectives are the things that matter to us. He is the picture that we have drawn, for good or ill, of ourselves.

Nothing is so important to the citizen as the way he helps in the drawing of this composite photograph—the way he chooses his leader and the kind of man he picks.

*   *   *

FOOTNOTES

[1] The leader must know that politics is the science of the possible. He must be able to view his objective in light of the total situation. He must correctly gauge the strength of the several viewpoints and interests concerned. Since his task is to provide a substitute for violence, to relieve social tension, and to promote harmony, he will find that "compromise" is his watch-word. He will understand that, in peacetimes at least, a 100 per cent correct position is not for him. He will

be thinking of the 40 per cent, the 60 per cent, or the 80 per cent position as the attainable one, and the 100 per cent vantage point as beyond the realm of the possible in democratic politics. This is because he will know that it is a condition that confronts him and not a theory—and a variety of people with free wills make up this condition.

[2] He said, in part:

"To the Congress of the United States:

"Unhappy events abroad have retaught us two simple truths about the liberty of a democratic people.

"The first truth is that the liberty of a democracy is not safe if the people tolerate the growth of private power to a point where it becomes stronger than their democratic state itself. That, in its essence, is fascism—ownership of government by an individual, by a group, or by any other controlling private power.

"The second truth is that the liberty of a democracy is not safe if its business system does not provide employment and produce and distribute goods in such a way as to sustain an acceptable standard of living.

"Both lessons hit home.

"Among us today a concentration of private power without equal in history is growing. . . .

I. THE GROWING CONCENTRATION OF ECONOMIC POWER

". . . The year 1929 was a banner year for distribution of stock ownership.

"But in that year three-tenths of 1 per cent of our population received 78 per cent of the dividends reported by individuals. This has roughly the same effect as if, out of every 300 persons in our population, 1 person received 78 cents out of every dollar of corporate dividends while the other 299 persons divided up the other 22 cents between them.

"The effect of this concentration is reflected in the distribution of national income.

"A recent study by the National Resources Committee shows that in 1935–36—

" 'Forty-seven per cent of all American families and single individuals living alone had incomes of less than $1,000 for the year; and at the other end of the ladder a little less than 1½ per cent of the Nation's families received incomes which in dollars and cents reached the same total as the incomes of the 47 per cent at the bottom.' . . .

"We believe in a way of living in which political democracy and free private enterprises for profit should serve and protect each other —to insure a maximum of human liberty not for a few but for all.

"It has been well said that, 'The freest government, if it could exist, would not be long acceptable if the tendency of the laws were to create a rapid accumulation of property in few hands, and to render the great mass of the population dependent and penniless.'

II. FINANCIAL CONTROL OVER INDUSTRY

". . . Private enterprise is ceasing to be free enterprise and is becoming a cluster of private collectivisms; masking itself as a system of free enterprise after the American model, it is in fact becoming a concealed cartel system after the European model.

"We all want efficient industrial growth and the advantages of mass production. No one suggests that we return to the hand loom or hand forge. A series of processes involved in turning out a given manufactured product may well require one or more huge mass-production plants. Modern efficiency may call for this. But modern efficient mass production is not furthered by a central control which destroys competition between industrial plants each capable of efficient mass production while operating as separate units. Industrial efficiency does not have to mean industrial empire building. . . .

"Business enterprise needs new vitality and the flexibility that comes from the diversified efforts, independent judgments and vibrant energies of thousands upon thousands of independent businessmen.

"The individual must be encouraged to exercise his own judgment and to venture his own small savings, not in stock gambling but in new enterprise investment. Men will dare to compete against men but not against giants.

III. THE DECLINE OF COMPETITION AND ITS EFFECTS ON EMPLOYMENT

"In output per man or machine we are the most efficient industrial nation on earth.

"In the matter of complete mutual employment of capital and labor we are among the least efficient.

"Our difficulties of employing labor and capital are not new. We have had them since good, free land gave out in the West at the turn of the century. They were old before we undertook changes in our tax policy or in our labor and social legislation. They were caused not by this legislation but by the same forces which caused the legislation. The problem of bringing idle men and idle money together will not be solved by abandoning the forward steps we have taken to adjust the burdens of taxation more fairly and to attain social justice and security. . . .

"One of the primary causes of our present difficulties lies in the disappearance of price competition in many industrial fields, particularly in basic manufacture where concentrated economic power is most evident and where rigid prices and fluctuating pay rolls are general. . . .

"Most complaints for violations of the antitrust laws are made by businessmen against other businessmen. Even the most monopolistic businessman disapproves of all monopolies but his own. We may smile at this as being just an example of human nature, but we cannot laugh away the fact that the combined effect of the monopolistic controls which each business group imposes for its own benefit inevitably destroys the buying power of the Nation as a whole.

"But generally over the field of industry and finance we must revive and strengthen competition if we wish to preserve and make workable our traditional system of free private enterprise.

"The justification of private profit is private risk. We cannot safely make America safe for the businessman who does not want to take the burdens and risks of being a businessman.

IV. THE CHOICE BEFORE US

". . . A discerning magazine of business has editorially pointed out that big-business collectivism in industry compels an ultimate collectivism in government. . . .

"The enforcement of free competition is the least regulation business can expect. . . .

"To meet the situation I have described, there should be a thorough study of the concentration of economic power in American industry and the effect of that concentration upon the decline of competition. There should be an examination of the existing price system and the price policies of industry to determine their effect upon the general level of trade, upon employment, upon long-term profits, and upon consumption. The study should not be confined to the traditional antitrust field. The effects of tax, patent, and other Government policies cannot be ignored. . . .

"(6) *Tax correctives*—Tax policies should be devised to give affirmative encouragement to competitive enterprise. . . .

"It is true that the form of the 1936 tax worked a hardship on many of the smaller corporations. Many months ago I recommended that these inequities be removed. . . .

"No man of good faith will misinterpret these proposals. They derive from the oldest American traditions. Concentration of economic power in the few and the resulting unemployment of labor and capital are inescapable problems for a modern 'private enterprise' democracy. I do not believe that we are so lacking in stability that we will lose faith in our own way of living just because we seek to find out how to make the way of living work more effectively.

"This program should appeal to the honest common sense of every independent businessman interested primarily in running his own business at a profit rather than in controlling the business of other men.

"It is not intended as the beginning of any ill-considered 'trust-busting' activity which lacks proper consideration for economic results.

"It is a program to preserve private enterprise for profit by keeping it free enough to be able to utilize all our resources of capital and labor at a profit.

"It is a program whose basic purpose is to stop the progress of collectivism in business and turn business back to the democratic competitive order.

"It is a program whose basic thesis is not that the system of free private enterprise for profit has failed in this generation, but that it has not yet been tried.

"Once it is realized that business monopoly in America paralyzes the system of free enterprise on which it is grafted, and is as fatal to those who manipulate it as to the people who suffer beneath its impositions, action by the Government to eliminate these artificial restraints will be welcomed by industry throughout the Nation.

"For idle factories and idle workers profit no man."

[3] Hearings available through the Superintendent of Documents, Government Printing Office, Washington, D.C.

Part 1. Economic Prologue—December 1, 2, and 3, 1938
General Economic Statements by Messrs. Lubin, Thorp and Henderson.

Part 2. Automobile patent hearings—December 5 and 6, 1938; also Glass container patent hearings—December 12, 13, 14, 15, and 16, 1938
Evidence of the use of patents in these industries.

Part 3. Patent hearings—January 16, 17, 18, 19 and 20, 1939
General data on patents as presented by Conway P. Coe, Commissioner of Patents.

Part 4. Insurance hearings—February 6, 7, 8, 9, 10, 14, 15, 16, and 17, 1939
Testimony on the size, growth, holdings, operating practices and other general information on insurance companies.

Part 5. Monopolistic practices in industries, presented by the Federal Trade Commission—February 28; March 1, 2, 3, 6, 7, 8, and 14, 1939; also
Development of the Beryllium Industry, presented by the Department of Justice—May 8 and 9, 1939, including testimony on the international exchange of patent rights.

Part 5A. Federal Trade Commission report on Monopolistic practices in industries—March 2, 1939
Case studies by the FTC of monopolistic practices.

Part 6. Liquor industry hearings—March 14, 15, 16, and 17, 1939

Testimony on the ownership, financing operations and sales practices in the liquor industry.

Part 7. Federal Trade presentation on monopolistic practices in the milk and poultry industries—March 9 and 10, 1939, including reports by the Federal Trade Commission; also rebuttal testimony regarding the milk industry—May 1, 2, and 3, 1939.

Part 8. Hearings on consumer problems as presented by Consumers' Counsel of the Agricultural Adjustment Administration—May 10, 11, and 12, 1939.

Part 10A. SEC report on "Operating results and investments of the twenty-six largest legal reserve life insurance companies in the U.S., 1929-1938."

Parts 9 and 10 will be listed as soon as they become available for distribution.

Also see: "Capital Not Wanted" and "Shadow over Wall Street" by Stuart Chase in the February and March, 1940, *Harper's;* "Let Business Roll Its Own" by Emmett F. Connely in the May, 1940, *Harper's;* "If You Were President" by Stuart Chase in the July 15, 1940, *New Republic;* and "Men First, Money Second" by Stuart Chase in the July 22, 1940, *New Republic.*

[4] Mr. Willkie's rise to national attention has been meteoric. It is partially indicated by the fact that his name did not appear in the *New York Times* in 1930, 1931, 1932, and appeared only once in 1933, seven times in 1934, 21 times in 1935, 16 times in 1936, 29 times in 1937, 39 times in 1938, 65 times in 1939, and 36 times during the first months of 1940. (This data was prepared for me by my student, Mr. John Heck.)

[5] "We the People—A Foundation for a Political Platform for Recovery," *Fortune,* April, 1940.

CHAPTER VI
CONCLUSIONS

My conclusions? You have them already. I have given them as I have gone along. The only conclusions that are really important in the democratic process are your own—the people's conclusions. Each one living under a free government not only can, but must, form his own conclusions. Do not let some professor tell you that he can do it for you. For he can't. My book is inadequate, I know. Yet I sincerely hope that I have been of some help to you in this great matter. You know Samuel Butler said, "Life is the art of drawing sufficient conclusions from insufficient premises." So begin now.